Contents

Long Loan

This book is due for return on or before the last date shown below.

List of Contributors

Jeremy Cunningham is Headteacher of Carterton Community College in West Oxfordshire. He was a founder member of the Amnesty International Education Programme. From 1983 to 1987 he was Deputy Head at the Sutton Centre, in Sutton-in-Ashfield.

Malcolm Harper is Director of the United Nations Association of Great Britain and Northern Ireland. From 1963 to 1987 he worked with Oxfam as Field Director in Eastern Africa, Emergencies Officer, Communications Director, and more recently as Team Leader in Cambodia.

Derek Heater is a freelance writer currently working on the history of schemes for European unity. He was founder-chairman of the Politics Association and editor of its journal, *Teaching Politics*. He is the author of many publications on citizenship and education.

Elizabeth Hoodless is Executive Director of Community Service Volunteers. She is a Member of the Council of the Royal Institute of Public Administration and was Deputy Chairman of the Speaker's Commission on Citizenship.

Eileen Baglin Jones is Assistant Education Officer with the Oxfordshire County Council and was formerly Director of the Achievement Project. She was previously Senior Teacher at Burford Community College and leader of the Oxfordshire New Learning Initiative Project (the government-funded Lower Attaining Pupil Project).

Neville Jones is a Regional Tutor in Special Needs at the Open University. He was Principal Education Psychologist with the Oxfordshire County Council Education Department from 1976 to 1990. During this period he directed the Oxfordshire Disaffected Pupil Programme and was the editor of a series of books on education and alienation.

Roy Manley is a management consultant to voluntary organizations. His previous posts include Assistant Adviser on Secondary Education to the Federal Nigerian Government, Research Manager and Secretary of The Acton Society Trust, Secretary-General of International Voluntary Service and Deputy Director of The National Council for Voluntary Organisations.

Jon Nuttall is Director of Studies and Head of Computing at St John's School in Leatherhead. He tutors in philosophy for the Open University.

Patricia Rogers is Head of the Council for Education in World Citizenship. In 1987 she was United Kingdom Co-ordinator of the 1988 campaign on north–south interdependence and solidarity, which included 200 events and 100 organizations, aimed at increasing awareness of the interdependence between developing and developed countries.

Don Rowe is Director of the Citizenship Foundation in London. He was previously Director of the Law in Education (11–14) Project.

Hugh Starkey is Principal Lecturer and Co-ordinator for European Affairs at Westminster College, Oxford. He is external examiner for the Diploma in Global and Multicultural Education at the University of York and a trustee of the World Studies Trust.

Sally Tomlinson is Professor of Education at London University, having previously been Professor of Education at Lancaster University. She is the author of a number of books on multicultural education.

Introduction

Eileen Baglin Jones and Neville Jones

Those who have recently addressed the issue of citizenship in education are alert to the contrasting and competing claims within a complicated set of ideas and ideals. In the foreword to *Encouraging Citizenship*, the Report of the Speaker's Commission on Citizenship (1990), the then Speaker of the House of Commons, the Right Hon. Bernard Weatherill, MP, reminded readers that a significant step forward in 'the long process of establishing a free society for men and women here in Britain' began with the enshrining of 'liberties, rights and concessions' as laid out in Magna Carta in 1215. The Speaker goes on to say: 'I believe that citizenship, like anything else, has to be learned. Young people do not become good citizens by accident. . .' This places *citizenship* centrally in the curriculum of our schools, enabling young people to be aware of and alert to the customs, rights, privileges, duties and responsibilities they have as members of a society, long before they become active and voting participants in a democracy.

The Commission focused its work on the teaching of citizenship in schools. The National Curriculum Council Report *Education for Citizenship* (NCC, 1990), which followed in the footsteps of the Commission's publication, declared that 'citizenship should be one of the five cross-curriculum themes that schools should take into account'. The Education Reform Act of 1988, in the restructuring proposals for a new National Curriculum, had included Education for Citizenship as one of the five themes located as cross-curriculum elements to ensure a 'broad and balanced' school curriculum. But all these declarations of intent have not dispelled anxieties about the politicizing of the school curriculum and the danger of a government, heavily centralized in the control of state education services, using the Education for Citizenship option to promote its own political values. Some members of Parliament already see citizenship studies as part of a widely based pressure for Britain to have a Bill of Rights. The resistance to such developments finds expression in legislation and government reports. Jim Sweetman, Chief Executive for the General Certificate of Secondary Education examinations, has drawn attention to the fact that 'in the guidance issued by the National Curriculum Council describing Education for Citizenship the word "rights" never appears on its own'. In relation to work and employment the reference is always to 'rights and duties'; in being a citizen to 'rights and privileges'. Sweetman notes that under the section headed 'The Citizen and the Law', there is no mention of rights at all! It is not so long ago that a former Prime Minister cast doubt on whether something we might call 'society' even exists – even though at the time her Ministers were preparing education legislation to ensure that the curriculum in schools promoted 'spiritual, moral, cultural, mental and physical development of pupils at school and *in society*. . .'.

The fact that Education for Citizenship studies are located as a cross-curriculum theme poses anxieties for those favouring such studies, and very practical logistical problems for school curriculum planners as to where, in the timetable, such a subject will find a place and be accorded a suitable value and meaning. The proposal by the NCC that cross-curriculum themes should, in some as yet undefined way, find a place by being filtered into the main subjects of the National Curriculum suggests that those themes have low government priority. Demands are now being made on teachers arising from the National Curriculum, involving testing, assessment and evaluation of pupils at regular intervals, and there are problems of staff morale and recruitment. Cross-curriculum themes may lack credibility because, unlike the foundation subjects, they have not been accorded legitimate assessment structures. All this means that teachers will be somewhat taxed in finding a way to teach citizenship studies, if these studies are to compete with other core and foundation subjects.

Clayton Mackenzie, Assistant Dean and Head of Education at St Mary's College, Twickenham, has declared that 'the cross-curriculum dimensions of a school's curriculum must be timetabled mainly *outside* the foundation subject areas. If cross-curricular aspirations of the National Curriculum are to find significant fulfilment, it will be through whole-school or whole-year-group projects, afforded effective preparation–performance structure, and not through cross-curricular threads, however well some may hope they will be woven into already voluminous subject fabrics.' Such approaches can be developed even further. Jeremy Cunningham explores the idea that education in citizenship, its values and opportunities, is a method whereby a school can offer its pupils *active* experience in citizenship responsibilities, by virtue of participatory activities of staff and pupils. He describes in Chapter 10 the work that is being developed at Carterton Community College, along 'citizenship' lines, to promote a school management structure with a particular value system and ethos. And he describes how citizenship skills can be acquired simply by being a participating member of an institution and society we call school.

If we accept that one of the main aims of education is to help young people to become aware of themselves as valued, autonomous and responsible individuals – such awareness being a prerequisite for effective learning – it seems to follow that this cannot happen in a vacuum. 'No man [or woman] is an island' . . . we all have to learn how to live and work and interact with other people in the circles of society beyond our immediate family group. To do this successfully one must be actively involved. In this sense 'actively involved' means 'engaged in' or 'committed to' an idea, an area of interest or a project. This was expressed by Speaker Weatherill, in his foreword, as follows:

> . . . young people at the outset of their adult lives need to be offered this *experience* of working with others to tackle and solve real problems in their own local environment. I believe that that kind of experience of involvement, of belonging, of sharing responsibility, is a crucial element in the process of learning to be a good citizen.

THE CONCEPT OF CITIZENSHIP

In such a simple statement of intent it is already possible to see how different interpretations are being placed on such seemingly straight-forward concepts as *active* and *voluntary*, and indeed, the term *citizenship* itself. Hugh Starkey explores these differences in this book, in his chapter on citizenship studies and practice in France. 'Participation' for the English child almost invariably means services to the local community and knowing where needs exist and where contributions can be made. It is because of such basic difficulties, about language and concepts, that the Commission spent time on examining the definition of the term 'citizenship'. Drawing on the work of political philosophers and current theorists like Hannah Arendt and Sir Ralf Dahrendorf, the Commission utilized the work of T H Marshall (*Citizenship and Social Class*, 1950) in an attempt to focus their work in a way that would lead to practical ways of developing citizenship studies. It is because of confusions surrounding the term that the opening chapter of this book, by Derek Heater, sets out to explore what these might be in a historical sense: first, by examining the differences between the liberal and republican traditions in the theory and practice of citizenship; secondly, the issue of state allegiances and multiple citizenship; and thirdly, how crucial the role of citizenship is, both for the individual and the state. Derek Heater then relates this background of theory and practice to present-day statements and publications as these relate to the teaching of citizenship in schools – and the tensions that invariably arise.

Active participation appears to be a key theme in all the publications to date. The Commission report draws attention to the fact that 'the right to participate in the exercise of political power, as a member of a body invested with political authority or as an elector of the members of a central body, is a central entitlement of each citizen in a democracy . . . the exercise of such rights is tied up with the question of legal membership of the political community.' The report then details some of the obstacles to participation and where these problems lie: the under-representation of women in Parliament, in the Honours system, on the management boards of businesses, and in the trade union movement; the number of women councillors active in local and central government; the problems of appointing Justices of the Peace in order to reflect a social balance in society; the lack of commitment to services for the socially disadvantaged; and anomalies in the field of social benefits.

Central to active participation in Great Britain is the work of the voluntary organizations – 'self-governing bodies of people who have joined together voluntarily to take action for the benefit of the community and have been established otherwise than for financial gain' (National Council for Voluntary Organizations, 1990). It was at the instigation of one of these bodies (Community Service Volunteers) that the Commission on citizenship came into being. It seems only appropriate, therefore, that the Executive Director of that organization, who was also Deputy Chairman of the Commission, should contribute to this book. Chapter 4 outlines the work of the CSV, which since 1962 has involved over three million 'active citizens'.

The relationship of voluntary organizations to the state depends to some extent upon whether the voluntary body is registered as a charity. The latter are bound by the law and have to confine their activities within the rules and objectives of their trusts. Roy Manley, from his position as a management consultant to voluntary organizations and former Secretary-General of International Voluntary Service, is well placed to appraise the difficulties and the context within which voluntary organizations work. He traces the history of charitable action in this country from the days of the early church to the present, when voluntary organizations are more locked into the work of public services, and with increasing emphasis on community rather than institutional care. If a voluntary organization is to take a political stance it has to take good care to do this within the constitutional limits of its own objectives. Manley further points out that 'a voluntary organization should take pains not to be *party* political, i.e., not to come out in support of a particular party that it might see as more sympathetic to its objectives.' These are areas for discretionary attitudes and behaviours, bearing in mind that charities can obtain a measure of tax relief and a charity can seek money from those foundations whose constitutions forbid grants to non-charities. Great power, therefore, is invested in such government bodies as the Charity Commissioners.

ACTIVE CITIZENSHIP

In general, there is less anxiety generated by the idea of 'volunteer action', even if it does in some circumstances result in direct political activity, than in the notice of 'active citizenship'. This then raises the questions of how far we expect young people to be politically 'active' and to what extent institutions of the state, like state schools, should be mediators for this kind of education. An interesting parallel has been drawn by Hugh Starkey in his account of citizenship education in France (Chapter 6). He draws attention to the 'localized' form of citizenship 'teaching' and activity in English Schools – for example, related to local community services, needs, and activities. The French, however, seem to stress 'citizenship' in terms of symbols and mottoes – learning about 'the President and parliament . . . democracy, human rights . . . and political and institutional aspects of national life'. English primary-age children 'are not expected to learn about the Queen nor Her Majesty's Government and Armed Forces. There is no mention of the flag, nor of the national anthem . . . and no formal attempt is made to explain and perhaps justify the monarchy . . . English children are shielded from such matters.' At secondary level the syllabus guidelines for English students 'lack the extensive study of human rights documents and texts and the specifically anti-racist position taken by the French official guidance'. Starkey wonders how the avoidance of political discussion and controversial issues provides English students with an effective syllabus that would prepare them to be informed citizens supporting a democracy.

Some further comparisons are interesting: the French guidelines make reference to human rights organizations, while the English syllabus lists youth organizations (the work of Guides, Scouts, Outward Bound, and Operation Raleigh) and first aid (Red Cross and St John Ambulance). The police are not mentioned in the French syllabus but the National Curriculum Council's publication *Education for Citizenship* notes that 'the contribution of the police services is of the greatest importance, especially the involvement of the school community liaison officers in lessons and extracurricular activities' (p. 13).

Patricia Rogers, in her contribution (Chapter 7) on education as this relates to international responsibilities of citizenship, extends the society we live in. She reminds us that, while every society is concerned about its constituent members, so each society has duties and obligations that extend beyond society groups, and she gives examples of this from the European Community, NATO and the Commonwealth. This linking between member states, providing full citizenship rights to all people, was enshrined in the Universal Declaration of Human Rights, adopted by the General Assembly of the United Nations in 1948. This Declaration covered social, political and civil rights. In discussing these areas Patricia Rogers extends the discussion to a natural consideration of how it is possible to develop the skills of citizenship and of the importance of training for the teacher of international understanding, co-operation and peace, related to human rights and fundamental freedom.

The international perspective is also well extended in Malcolm Harper's account (Chapter 8) of the work of the United Nations, of which he has a wide experience and about which he speaks with authority, particularly concerning UN activities over recent years. There was a time when the United Nations was considered, in the words of one newspaper columnist, as:

> a mass of antediluvian arrangements, antique special interests, entrenched groups, sacred conventions and untouchable procedures. . . . Its assembly is the most hidebound, predictable and ineffective of the world's parliaments.

Whatever the merits of that appraisal, the United Nations has from time to time provided a service across nations, set out precisely in Malcolm Harper's chapter, so that there is now a greater expectation that this world body can play a greater and consistently beneficial role in world affairs. The organization that the Secretary-General of the UN, Boutros Ghali, has inherited from Perez de Cuellar is beginning to play an increased role in world conflicts, with an increasingly wide-ranging set of expectations.

At the moment we are experiencing an 'optimistic' period in the life of the United Nations, and as such it is an important time to engage the interest and participation of young students, involving such issues as drug-trafficking, the destruction of the South American rainforests, and the conflicts in Cambodia. These are topics that were covered at a Model United Nations General Assembly (MUNGA) meeting for 150 fifth- and sixth-form students from Oxfordshire secondary schools and colleges. Such meetings represent part of the work being carried out in Oxfordshire LEA schools, and are described by the editors of this book in more detail in Chapter 9. For the second meeting of the MUNGA, in 1992, students were scheduled to take on board a fuller set of issues: global warming, refugees, population and the international transfer of arms. A simulation exercise of this kind, supported by the United Nations Association of Great Britain through the good offices of their Director, Malcolm Harper, requires the students to know more about the countries that they are to represent. A possible consequence of this is to inform students about the views the countries have on the issues under discussion, leading to a better understanding of the country's culture and how different nations approach a problem from quite different starting-points. The occasion also helps the students to inform themselves better on the issues to be debated: apart from library studies, they are expected to contact embassy staff for material, and to issue invitations to visit the schools. Students have to remember on the day that, whatever their own opinions and prejudices, they are there to express the views of the country they represent. This has proved for some to be more than just an exercise in mental gymnastics. During the afternoon of the first MUNGA meeting the Foreign Secretary, Douglas Hurd, led a discussion on all three topics on the UN agenda, and provided some background information on the workings of the United Nations from his own informed position, as a delegate to the UN and later as Foreign Secretary. As this meeting took place during the week that Mrs Thatcher resigned as Prime Minister, the students also had a glimpse of the national press at work in the political arena!

If there is confusion and antagonism over the term 'active citizenship', there is even more when this concept is considered in terms of a citizen's rights, duties and obligations. Dahrendorf takes the view that rights – civil, political, and social – are a precise concept. Civil rights entail equality before the law, the due process of justice, and the right to conclude contracts as equals – that is, the rule of law in its widest sense. Political rights include the right to vote and to express one's views. Social rights in part embrace civil and political rights – they liberate people from insecurity, and include the right to an education and the right not to fall below a certain level of income. Dahrendorf believes that much of the discussion about individual rights has led to a backlash in capitalist societies, so that rights are discussed only in a context of obligations. This, he believes, has led to the intervention of 'active citizenship', which in essence means that citizens should not only be self-interested (make money) but have an obligation towards others (which in political terms in a capitalist society means giving money for public purposes). Dahrendorf is not against philanthropy but views the debate on this as incidental to the issue of citizenship, which for him is an embodiment of rights and entitlements for people. Clearly there are obligations such as obeying the law and paying taxes: but we should not place our rights as citizens at risk simply because we do not fulfil citizenship obligations. Rights have an absolute value, so these are to be protected and are not to be qualified by, for example, not paying the poll tax. The Commission on Citizenship supports Dahrendorf in the position he takes on rights and duties, but clearly, in its Report, is more taxed by the question of obligations.

In his chapter Don Rowe raises issues concerned with the teaching of rights and duties of citizenship, and the law through which these are mediated. He rightly draws attention to the complexity inherent in the relationship between an individual and the community in which the individual lives and has rights grounded in legislation: a complexity that goes beyond factual knowledge where the teaching of 'citizenship' in schools is concerned. Learning about citizenship has both a 'cognitive and experiential' aspect and for younger children the learning about their local community carries a greater immediacy than knowledge focused on events national or international. Teaching citizenship, therefore, is a changing process for the individual child, with different emphasis as the child becomes aware of, and possibly experiences, the wider implications of being a member of a community or state, and of one state among many others worldwide. There has been very little taught in schools about rights and duties, and the ways these find expression in the legal framework of a state, and it has been assumed that matters legal were the prerogative of an academic elite. There have been no syllabuses constructed with the 'aim of addressing the real needs of citizens'.

Sally Tomlinson has looked in detail at an area where difficulties about rights arise, namely, minority groups. The issues take on greater importance when we think of the demands of the neo-Nazis in Germany to exclude immigrants, of Le Pen's political drive in France to rid the country of Arabs (and in the interim remove their rights as citizens), and in Britain in the ever increasing legislation to prohibit immigration and narrow the definition of political refugees. Dahrendorf picks up the issue of multicultural nationality and international citizenship. He regards it as illogical to preach and practise citizenship in terms of a set of rights and entitlements while excluding from it those who have their origins in other countries but choose to opt for citizenship in Britain. Included, of course, among these 'strangers in our midst' are those who have secured British nationality or have been born of those whose residence allows them to be regarded as British. The question of multiple identity is one that is also discussed by Derek Heater in Chapter 1. He loooks at the idea of citizens having both a national and multiple citizenship and sees this as becoming increasingly necessary. He concludes: 'what is needed is a clarification and simplification of the law, both municipal and international, so that the individual can easily understand the rights and duties that attach to each role.' Tomlinson, in her contribution on minority groups (Chapter 2), offers a detailed analysis of what has happened to non-white immigrants to Britain, where 'minorities from former colonial countries, encouraged by the state to migrate to work in Britain, have faced a 40-year struggle to acquire and to exercise their political, civil and social citizenship rights. They have also faced a white majority seemingly determined to reject non-white groups as equal citizens within the British nation.' She reminds her readers that the Swann Report of 1985 'envisaged Britain as a plural democracy in which the rights and obligations of all communities towards each other should be defined, protected and respected – with education playing a key role in the process ... in the 1990s the claims of non-white groups to be full citizens and part of the British nation are still suspect, and multicultural education is derided as left-wing ideology. . .'. Tomlinson seeks to find the source of political resistance to the full integration of minority groups in the crisis that now exists in Britain concerning national identity and the way that nationalism finds an expression in the education service; and to seek solutions so that cultural and ethnic diversity can be seen as a valuable and not problematic issue for an integrated citizenship.

The final chapter in this book links up with many of the issues raised in Sally Tomlinson's chapter. Religious tolerance is a central theme for the integration of minority groups into a society, and Jon Nuttall raises some particularly difficult issues where religious belief and moral practice are concerned. This is particularly so in any country that has pretensions to multinational integration. Nuttall examines how it is possible to procure a moral education that explicitly includes religious teaching for the majority and, by definition, excludes religious teaching for the minority – especially if pupils from both cultures are to be involved in an integrated system of education. He analyses the way this problem has been dealt with through the Education Reform Act and how attempts have been made to accommodate moral teaching within a religious education formula. Nuttall argues that religious education (RE) cannot provide 'a moral framework for those pupils who do not share the religious beliefs on which it is based'. The way through this dilemma is by means of a form of philosophical teaching that does not conflict with Christian teachings.

The aim of this book has been to bring together the collective thoughts and experiences of a group of scholars, researchers and educational practitioners, to tease out some of the issues arising from a need to promote active citizenship education in our schools. It was hoped that contributors would be able to translate their expertise into ideas and proposals for those who have the task of implementing the curriculum, national or otherwise, in the classrooms. Teaching about citizenship is still an infant skill, a subject of which there are many facets and understandings. In this book the ground has been covered by chapters on principles and theory, the specific problems for minority groups, the work of voluntary groups, citizenship as practised overseas and through the work of the United Nations, and examples of how citizenship studies might be advanced through cross-curriculum management and whole-school policy and ethos. Even one of these areas, studied and interpreted in attitudes or practical experience, could provide opportunities for students to participate as better-informed and better-equipped members of society, able to offer more to the community in which they live.

REFERENCES

Dahrendorf, Sir R (1990) 'Decade of the Citizen', *The Guardian*, 1st August 1990.

Jones, N (1990) *Special Educational Needs Review (Integration)*, vol. 3, London: Falmer Press.

Marshall, T H (1950) *Citizenship and Social Class*, Cambridge University Press.

National Council for Voluntary Organizations (1990) *Effectiveness and the Voluntary Sector – Report of the Working Party*, London: NCVO.

National Curriculum Council (1990) *Curriculum Guidance 8: Education for Citizenship*, York: NCC.

Speaker's Commission on Citizenship (1990) *Encouraging Citizenship*, London: HMSO.

Part One: The Citizenship Perspective

Chapter 1

Tensions in the Citizenship Ideal

Derek Heater

INCOMPATIBILITIES

The purpose of education is the individual development of the child. The purpose of education is to fit the individual for community life in the state of which he or she is a member. The purpose of education is to render the individual sensitive to societies beyond his or her own country, including the global community. All these pedagogical objectives are sincerely and justifiably held. But are they mutually compatible? Or would the simultaneous pursuit of these aims generate unbearable educational, not to mention political, tensions?

Of all the thinkers who have struggled to square such unmalleably round circles, Rousseau worried most about these particular social and political issues. It is fitting therefore briefly to outline his views on the question. In *Émile*, that most famous book of educational advice, he pointed to the stark alternatives:

> Consistency is plainly impossible when we seek to educate a man for others, instead of for himself. If we have to combat either nature or society, we must choose between making a man or making a citizen. We cannot make both. (Boyd, 1956, p. 13.)

The prevailing message is that Émile should be educated 'to develop his own tastes, his own talents, to take the first step towards the object which appeals to his individuality' (Macfarlane, 1970, p. 154).

In other moods Rousseau offered the contrary emphasis. In the *Discourse on Political Economy* he wrote of the benefits that would be derived if men 'were early accustomed to regard their individuality only in its relation to the body of the State, and to be aware, so to speak, of their own existence merely as a part of the State' (Macfarlane, 1970, p. 195). Similarly, in his *Considerations on the Government of Poland*, he wrote that 'it is education which must shape their minds in the national mould

... till they are patriotic by inclination – by instinct – by necessity' (Curtis and Boultwood, 1956, p. 267).

But was this education for civic identity to be focused only on the state? Rousseau was, of course, particularly enamoured of the city-state, while at the same time conscious of the sentiment that was coming to consolidate the nation-state. On the other hand, there were moments when he revealed an appreciation of the more extensive bonds of Europe and even of the world itself. In his *Abstract* of Saint-Pierre's *Perpetual Peace* he is at pains to emphasize that Europe is 'a real community with a religion and a moral code, with customs and even laws of its own' (Forsyth *et al.*, 1970, p. 135). And in the *Discourse on the Origin of Inequality* he writes of 'great Cosmopolitan Souls who cross the imaginary barriers which separate Peoples, and who . . . embrace all of Humanity in their benevolence' (Rousseau, 1969, p. 178). True, in neither of these works does he write of European or world citizenship, still less of education for either of those concepts. Indeed, to posit European or global dimensions to citizenship would have been a contradiction of the term 'citizenship' as he understood it as a clear political status. On the other hand, it is evident that he had a perception of a kind of communal identity that transcended the established state and that had some claim on the individual's sense of social responsibility.

The problem of apparent incompatibilities in the citizenship ideal is still very much with us today, nearly two and a half centuries after Rousseau. I propose to look at three major expressions of tension and their educational implications. The first topic is the difference between the 'liberal' and 'republican' traditions in the theory and practice of citizenship. The second is the difference between the belief that citizenship can properly exist only in relation to the state and the alternative idea that an individual can hold a multiple citizenship. The third question concerns the argument as to whether or not the role of citizenship is crucially important for the individual and the state.

'LIBERAL' VERSUS 'REPUBLICAN' TRADITIONS

In the words of Adrian Oldfield, there are two different conceptions of citizenship, which 'have different histories in the development of Western thought, and, more importantly, . . . have different conceptions themselves of the nature of the individual, and of the character of the social bonds existing between individuals as citizens (Oldfield, 1990, p. 177). He identifies these two traditions as the liberal–individualist and the civic–republican.

The liberal tradition of citizenship focuses on the freedom and rights of the individual. Citizenship is a status that has been striven for since the 17th century and in that process of struggle has been constantly extended in definition and application. The significance of this process has been the gradual emancipation of the individual's life from arbitrary state oppression and the steady enhancement of the rights of the individual *vis-à-vis* the state.

In their search for a lucid exposition of this interpretation of citizenship, recent commentators in Britain have latched on to T H Marshall's lectures on the topic, delivered in 1949. Marshall argued that citizenship properly consists of three sets of component rights, which have been acquired in Britain in roughly chronological sequence: civil, political and social. He defined these in the following way:

> The civil element is composed of the rights necessary for individual freedom – liberty of the person, freedom of speech, thought and faith, the right to own property and to conclude valid contracts, and the right to justice. . . . By the political element I mean the right to participate in the exercise of political power. . . . By the social element I mean the whole range from the right to a modicum of economic welfare and security to the right to share to the full in the social heritage and to live the life of a civilized being. . . . (Marshall, 1950, pp. 10–11.)

What are the implications of this liberal notion of citizenship? First we may note that citizenship, far from being a clear-cut status, is a relative term. It has been enjoyed in varying degrees by different individuals, in different places and at different times. Those who have fought for the ideal, believing in its value, have extended in piecemeal fashion the range of rights conceded and the number of individuals who have been able to enjoy them. The simplest illustration of this feature of citizenship is the gradual extension of the franchise.

However, and this is the second feature, all individuals are equal by the terms of the liberal definition of citizenship. Equal, that is, in the right to enjoy the rights. Reality may all too often be a very imperfect approximation to this ideal. But we must not lose sight of the egalitarian principle central to citizenship in its notional perfect form.

The third facet of the liberal idea of citizenship is the assumed tension between individual and state, most evidently during the process of consolidating the rights. The rights have to be extracted from the state and are necessary to defend the individual against the state.

On the other hand, and fourthly, once civil rights are in place in the laws and practices of the land, the individual has little need to exercise them. Good citizens should turn out to vote and dutifully pay their taxes. They should be comforted by the constant protection afforded by their civic rights, not discomfited by their exhausting exercise.

This very basic sketch of the liberal citizenship tradition nevertheless requires a supplementary note. Recent commentary in Britain – by the civic reform movement Charter 88, for example – has insisted that the price of citizenship is eternal struggle. The case proceeds along the following lines. If, as in the Thatcher years, 'the national interest' was an argument abused for the purpose of abridging civil rights; if the 'first-past-the-post' electoral system in effect politically disenfranchises millions of so-called citizens; if the neglect of the welfare state deprives the needy of their social rights; if all this is an accurate portrayal of Britain in the 1980s, then citizenship has been eroded. The age-old fight for the maintenance and extension of the liberal idea of citizenship must be continued.

But citizenship is far, far older than liberal individualism. The Greeks and Romans who developed the theory and practice of citizenship in the ancient world would have been most perplexed at the notion of its deployment *against* the state. The classical view of citizenship, on the contrary, revealed it as a status and set of duties borne with pride. For only by the individual's conscientious discharge of his civic responsibilities would he achieve full moral development and the state grow maturely distinct from a tyranny – in short, become a republic.

This conception of citizenship was revived in Renaissance Italy, most notably by Machiavelli; it underlay Rousseau's devotion to classical models and informed much of American political idealism, from the time of the revolution onwards. The key component in this tradition is imperfectly rendered by the modern English word 'virtue'. Bernard Crick has succinctly defined civic virtue as 'the qualities of endeavour, involvement and audacity which hold states together' (Crick, n.d., pp. 57–88).

The republican version of citizenship is thus more positive and dynamic than the liberal. A citizen in the republican tradition is unworthy of the title if he rests on the laurels of the rights acquired by the efforts of prior generations. A citizen is a citizen only by virtue of the public service he or she undertakes.

The style of republican thinking about citizenship may be indicated by reference to four characteristic features. One is the importance of a sense of community. The relationship of citizens to each other is as important as the relationship of the citizen to the state. Citizenship is the sharing of a common civic life. This is, of course, much easier on the smaller than the larger scale. This is why advocates of the republican style of citizenship often emphasize their preference for the city-state, as Rousseau did, or for engagement in local civic activity, as in the case of de Tocqueville.

However, no matter what size the state might be, the citizen is expected to display a fitting patriotism. This love of country, the second characteristic, would normally be expressed as enthusiastic loyalty. Sometimes it requires selfless loyalty; citizenship involves military service for the defence of the state.

Training and fighting as a soldier has been but one form of duty traditionally expected of the good citizen. The zealous engagement in civic duties generally is the third feature we should notice. True citizens place the performance of such duties at the very top of their list of priorities. Time and energy must be found for these commitments, before hobbies, even perhaps before one's family. The ultimate devotion to this code must even be to sacrifice one's family, as the consul Brutus, liberator of Rome from the Tarquins, so famously did in condemning his own sons to death for conspiring to restore the monarchy.[1]

Fourthly, underlying duty is honour. Corruption is unthinkable in a state suffused with the civic–republican spirit. Nor is 'free-riding' on the claimed rights of citizenship to be at all entertained. Duties are performed honestly and conscientiously. The republican style of citizenship is thus much sterner than the liberal.

THE STATE VERSUS MULTIPLE CITIZENSHIP

Citizenship is both a status and an attitude of mind. In both senses it has evolved historically and can be most simply expressed in terms of the relationship of the individual to the state. Few would dissent from the following as a brief definition of the term 'citizenship':

> Citizenship is a relationship between an individual and a state involving the individual's full political membership in the state and his permanent allegiance to it. . . . The status of citizen is official recognition of the individual's integration into the political system.[2]

The validity of such a definition may be demonstrated by a number of concrete examples.

In the first place, it is the state that confers the status and that can withdraw it. Thus in Britain the 1981 British Nationality Act specifies just who is a British citizen. Or rather, in this extraordinarily convoluted case, into which particular category of citizenship any given individual falls: British, British Overseas or British Dependent Territories citizen. The most common defining document of citizenship is the passport, issued by the state of which one is an acknowledged citizen. By the same token, the state can revoke the status of citizenship. This action has both a practical and symbolic purpose and was used against political dissidents in the Soviet Union and East European countries in the 1970s and 1980s particularly. The pronouncement of the withdrawal of the status is a breaking of the bond, a formal act of punishment by the state on its deviant citizen.

Secondly, it is in the context of the state that citizens exercise their rights and perform their duties. They elect their representatives to a national legislature; they serve on juries; they pay taxes; and the men are liable for conscripted military service. Insofar as the status of citizen is characterized by the civil, political and social rights outlined by Marshall, then those rights derive from state-enacted legislation.

From the Greek city-state to the present-day nation-state citizenship has been an attribute of the politically mature state. This is a matter of such obvious historical, legal and political fact as to need no further elaboration. On the other hand, the tradition has not been so powerful as utterly to preclude the idea or even practice of multiple citizenship.

Multiple citizenship may be conceived in three forms. The first need not detain us as it affects only a small number of people. It is the arrangement whereby an individual may, in law, have dual nationality – may be a citizen in an equal sense of two states.

The second form embraces the notion of world citizenship. An individual may think of him- or herself as holding world citizenship, with or without a simultaneous feeling of allegiance to the state of which he or she is a citizen. Again, little need be said of this concept here because another essay in this collection deals specifically with this ideal. What we do need to emphasize is that the status can only be self-proclaimed, albeit with utmost sincerity; it is not a legal status. The Stoics of ancient Greece and Rome and the men of the 18th-century Enlightenment would call themselves 'world citizens' merely in the sense of wishing to obey a natural law of good human conduct. Citizenship as a legal status can be conferred only by a state and there never has been a world state. For this reason some purists would have it that 'world citizenship' is at worst semantic nonsense, at best a metaphor. These comments are meant in no way to deride the notion of a world commitment, merely to emphasize the limitations of the term 'world citizenship' in comparison with state citizenship.

The third kind of multiple citizenship is the pyramidal or concentric form found in states with a federal structure. Thus an inhabitant of Munich is a citizen of the *Land* of Bavaria as well as of the state of Germany. Certain rights and duties adhere to the former status, others to the latter. However, it is recognized that in any serious conflict of interests the citizen's allegiance to the overarching state would take precedence over that owed to the provincial or local. Not that the relative strengths of these bonds necessarily remain the same over a period of time. Professor Murray Forsyth has demonstrated the interesting historical tendency of loose confederations to develop into tighter federations (Forsyth, 1981). This happened in the Netherlands, Switzerland, the USA and Germany. In this evolution prime loyalty and exercise of citizenship gradually shift from the constituent states to the federal state.

Now these observations are especially pertinent to the recent and possible future continued political integration of the European Community. In what senses, we may already ask, are those of us who live in the twelve member-states even now 'European' (or more strictly 'community') citizens?

European citizenship has been and still is evolving. This evolutionary process has been the result of two forces: one is the urge to greater integration beyond a mere trading common market; the other is the belief that this process should involve popular participation, not just bureaucratic administration. However, the status of European citizenship is currently founded on a series of unrelated ad hoc laws and arrangements. For example, we now vote directly for our MEPs; we may use a European passport; the Single European Act will open up employment rights; and to make us *feel* Europeans we have a Community flag and anthem.

It is difficult to forecast with any degree of accuracy the speed with which further political union will be agreed. What is fairly obvious is that it will fall short of a fully fledged federal United States of Europe for some time yet. The status and style of European citizenship need therefore to be consolidated with this in view. The status and feeling of citizenship will continue for the foreseeable future to adhere primarily to the nation-state. Yet the Community tier of citizenship must by no means be ignored. Indeed, there is considerable concern about the 'democratic deficit' in the Community, which can be amortized only by increased popular involvement beyond the formality of election of politicians to a powerless European parliament.

The citizens of the member-states need to be much more aware of their double status. In particular, they need to be made more conscious of the fact that in certain circumstances they appropriately act as citizens of a state and in others as citizens of the European Community. Patriots, of course, fear that the European will come to overwhelm the national; federalists fear that the development of the European will be inhibited by the obsolete power of the national. Guidance about balance between the two is urgently needed.

CITIZENSHIP VERSUS INDIVIDUALISM

In most discussions about citizenship its value to the individual and to the community is generally either taken for granted or asserted, rather than queried. For instance, the Speaker's Commission on Citizenship declared: 'We believe that citizenship is one of the most important concepts of modern political struggle and social development' (Speaker's Commission on Citizenship, 1990).

The case for the existence and exercise of citizenship to the fullest extent may be summarized briefly as follows. A state, of whatever size and complexity, requires for its strength and health the cohesion that derives from the allegiance of its inhabitants. If that allegiance is given spontaneously, freely and actively, then we may correctly say that those inhabitants are behaving in this regard as citizens. And the individuals themselves gain through this mature sense of political identity. Living in a politically ordered society is, as Rousseau argued, both a corrupting and a civilizing experience. True citizens are those who consciously strive to enhance the civilizing power of their state. Both state and citizen achieve moral growth in that process.

A much more common argument today concerns the importance of citizens' rights. According to this argument, the true badge of citizenship is the cluster of civil, political and social rights that have been acquired by the individual from the state, often by painful struggle during the course of many generations. The individual has clearly benefited from this emergence to the condition of citizen: in the 'pre-civic' condition the individual has lacked the very freedom, equality and justice which the status of citizen is designed to ensure. The state is also a beneficiary in this process. The alternative to a state founded on the citizenship relationship is one founded on privilege or faction or both – foundations that can be dangerously unstable.

But citizenship involves duties. Clearly the state benefits from the services freely (in both senses) given by the citizen body. The state benefits materially from citizens' voluntary activities, which would otherwise have to be paid for. The state also derives the advantage of cohesion from the integration of the citizenry into public affairs. The individual who discharges no citizenly duties is also the poorer. He or she will be wanting in that form of practical social education that civic experience, as J S Mill argued, so effectively supplies. And since the willing performance of duties is altruistic behaviour, this element of citizenship enhances the individual's moral development.

But is there not also danger to both the state and the individual in this constant harping on citizenship? The continual hankering after whole clusters of rights that can never be fully satisfied may generate disappointments that could sour into destabilizing political discontent. Even encouraging the performance of civic duties may not be all that prudent. How much might the state suffer from the activities of an army of incompetent busybodies? Nor, to continue this contrary argument, does the individual gain from citizenship except in the most minimal of ways. Civic participation is not natural. True human fulfilment lies in the cultivation of family life and, to speak candidly, one's garden.

British Conservative Party political thinking is not quite so restrictive. It does, however, in some moods confine citizenship virtually to patriotism and local voluntary work (or what we might call micro-citizenship). Its credo, published in 1976 as *The Right Approach*, reveals this attitude:

But we do not base our approach solely on the individual, on the view that the only role of society is to provide a framework of laws within which individual opportunities can flourish without becoming self-destructive. If we were to do this, a number of other things in which Conservatives believe – patriotism, loyalty, duty – would be meaningless. Man is an individual answerable to himself. But he is also a citizen, the member of a complex network of small communities which go to make up society – family, neighbourhood, church, voluntary organization, workplace, and so on. (O'Gorman, 1986, p. 225.)

The model presented here, of tensions in three pairs of contradictory aspects of citizenship, is something of a simplification. There are also tensions across these pairs. The committed patriotism of the republican tradition clashes with the concept of multiple citizenship. The zeal required by that tradition is also incompatible with the belief that individuals should as far as possible live the life of 'private citizens'. The notion of world citizenship, insofar as it is a tenable idea, emphasizes the need for a personal sense of global duties and responsibility, which sits awkwardly with the liberal emphasis on rights extracted from the state.

EDUCATION AND POLITICAL TENSIONS

The shuffling of these components of citizenship into patterns of contradictions is not just a philosophical game. If an individual is to be a citizen in any meaningful sense, he or she must learn about the apparent tensions so as to be able to understand and cope with them. The individual, in short, must be taught about these complexities. The problem of identifying, clarifying and perhaps even resolving the contradictions is a very practical and urgent matter for the teaching profession.

Political discussion about citizenship often focuses on a given element to the exclusion of its opposite in the pair. Either the contradictory alternative is ignored or it is dismissed as insignificant or untenable. A similarly blinkered approach to the problem is discernible in discussions on education for citizenship. Let us take a few examples.

The casualness of the liberal as distinct from the republican tradition of citizenship has been reflected in education. Teachers in the liberal style have taught 'Civics' to provide a certain basic understanding of how the system works; but few people have thought that there is any need to take the matter too seriously. Except, that is, until there is a threat to the comfortable status quo. In Britain the political establishment recognized that the democratic parliamentary system had to be protected against totalitarianism in the 1930s and against far left and especially far right propaganda in the 1970s. Teachers involved in the

Association for Education in Citizenship in the first period and in the Politics Association in the second could therefore be encouraged in their attempts at dispelling a political apathy or alienation in their pupils that was dangerous in the circumstances.

Those who hold to the republican view of citizenship cannot allow the development of proper civic attitudes to be left to chance. They know that citizenship is an unnatural, difficult task, yet crucially important. The individual must therefore be assiduously prepared for the role. To quote Oldfield again:

> The moral character which is appropriate for genuine citizenship does not generate itself; it has to be authoritatively inculcated. This means that minds have to be manipulated. People, starting with children, have to be taught what citizenship means for them, in a political community, in terms of duties it imposes upon them, and they have to be motivated to perform these duties. This is successful when they perceive that the interests of the community are also their own. . . (Oldfield, 1990, p. 164.)

Whether liberal or republican and under whatever label, education for citizenship has traditionally been education for state citizenship. Insofar as this kind of education has been encouraged, more often than not it has been for the purpose of strengthening the state; in other words, an education for conformity. In a work of comparative education published in the USA in 1965 the authors reported that 'each system tries to imbue the young, implicitly or explicitly, with its particular notions of authority, legitimacy, the role of the citizen, and of the good life; at the same time it tries to present negative interpretations of alien systems' (Kazamias and Massialas in Brennan, 1981, p. 5). Over the past century or so citizenship education has been part of nation-building.

Extending the purpose of citizenship education to a more geographically generous conception must take into account this strongly entrenched position. In Britain from the turn of the century to the 1960s schools were encouraged to teach pupils that they were members of the Empire, then of the Commonwealth. However, especially until about 1945, this was little more than a nationalist education writ large. A more serious challenge to the nationalist tradition is currently developing with the agreed need to give more prominence to the 'European dimension' in education in the member-states of the European Community. This includes the requirement that young people come to understand what it means to be a European citizen.[3]

'Education for world citizenship' is a phrase that gained currency in the early decades of the present century. It arose from the belief that young people should be brought up to look beyond their own nation-state, as a means of taming the dreadful urges that have led mankind into the horrendous world wars. The concept of education for world citizenship has added relevance today because of the widespread belief that young people must understand the fragile nature of the world's ecosystem.

There are still, nevertheless, a number of commentators who believe that education for citizenship of any kind is not a proper function for schools to undertake. Two main arguments have been marshalled in support of this negative view. One is that politics is an adult study unsuited to young people. Part of this argument is that it is in essence a practical activity, which can be understood only by engagement in it. The second argument is that the stuff of politics, about which it is the citizen's job to make judgments, is necessarily contentious. The handling of controversy in the classroom is dangerous because it can lead to heightened emotions, indoctrination by teachers and objections by parents.

On the other hand, the case in favour of education for citizenship is currently held in Britain to be much more powerful. Just as it is too hazardous to allow young people to pick up scraps of sex education behind the lavatories, so it is also too hazardous to allow them a few years later to pick up equally scrappy and distorted views about political and legal affairs in the pubs. Citizenship education is written into the National Curriculum as a required cross-curricular theme. But do the official documents that expound the theme get to grips with the tensions at its very heart?

CITIZENSHIP, TENSIONS AND THE NATIONAL CURRICULUM

In the late 1980s a government decision was taken to include Citizenship as a cross-curricular theme in the new National Curriculum for the schools of England and Wales. The key documents for the development of this theme are the Report of the Commission on Citizenship set up by the Speaker of the House of Commons[4] and the guidelines booklet produced by the National Curriculum Council.[5]

To start with the third of our tensions: it is scarcely likely that these documents, written to promote citizenship and the teaching of citizenship, will deny its importance. Both publications indeed go out of their way to emphasize its crucial importance. Thus the Speaker's Commission concludes its report by asserting that:

> Neglect of citizenship, of the entitlements and duties of individuals and obligations of institutions, and of the quality of participation can damage much that we value in our society.[6]

And when the Commission addressed the particular question of education they were equally forthright:

> The Commission strongly supports the case for citizenship studies to be part of every young person's education . . . from the earliest year of schooling and continuing into the post-school years within further and higher education and the youth service.[7]

The Chairman of the National Curriculum Council does not beat about the bush. The first sentence of his foreword to the guidance booklet states quite unequivocally: 'Education for citizenship is essential for every young pupil.'[8]

Here, then, are explicit rejections of the minimalist view of citizenship. Every child must be taught the citizen's role; every adult must conscientiously perform it. The tension between the active and passive styles of citizenship is resolved by simply ignoring the latter as a conceivable option. Young English citizens, like Rousseau's, must be forced to be free.

This would suggest that what the compilers of these documents have in mind is the republican rather than the liberal style of citizenship. Is this so? It is pertinent to remember that the Conservative Party's notion of 'active citizenship' in the late 1980s was a kind of bastard civic republicanism. It called for zealous participation, but of a very narrow social, politically emasculated kind. As the genesis of the government's keenness to encourage citizenship, especially in schools, lay in this active citizenship campaign, we might expect that it would shape the two key documents.

It is, however, clear that the authors of *Encouraging Citizenship* and *Curriculum Guidance 8* by no means reckoned that the idea of supplementary voluntary community help provided a complete definition. True, the report of the Speaker's Commission, which claims to provide a definitional starting-point, is in fact extraordinarily weak in its theoretical analysis. It relies heavily upon Marshall and seems unaware of the complexity of the concept beyond his delineation; and certainly unaware of the two streams of political thinking that have been characterized as civil republican and liberal individualist. As a result both the documents we are considering display elements from each tradition, but with no attempt to ensure that all the features of each are considered, or to test whether they are in any ways incompatible.

The liberal individualist coloration of *Encouraging Citizenship* derives in large measure from its heavy reliance on Marshall. This liberal tinge is reinforced by the way in which the report draws attention to various international human-rights documents: four of its eight appendices are devoted to these. And so when it comes to presenting evidence to the National Curriculum Council it is not surprising to find this style of thinking transmitted. For example, under the heading of 'Values and Attitudes' the paper points out that:

> The [European Community] Council of Ministers recommends that

the main [human rights] international charters and conventions to which the UK is signatory should provide the reference points, within the classroom, for the study of citizenship.[9]

Then, turning to 'Citizenship as a Body of Knowledge', the paper refers to the Commission's definition with its 'delineation of the civil, political and social entitlements and responsibilities. . . .'[10]

When we turn to the NCC document we read that the values that education for citizenship should promote are 'justice, democracy, respect for the rule of law'.[11] The emphasis on citizens' rights is to be found in the section entitled 'Content: the Essential Components'. Under the subheading 'Being a Citizen' we read the list: 'civil, political, social and human rights'. The gloss on duties and responsibilities is the need to promote 'respect for law' and 'to appreciate the need to protect the weak and disadvantaged'.[12]

Even so, there are traces of the civic–republican stance too. In the Report of the Speaker's Commission, two passages are particularly noteworthy. Under the subheading 'Ways of Encouraging Citizenship' we find the statement that 'If adequate support is to be made available to enable men and women to organize themselves, and influence decision-making locally and nationally, adult education and community development are of paramount importance.'[13] This sentence clearly speaks of an expectation of continuous political participation in the republican tradition. Later, on the topic of public attitudes, the document emphasizes the need for civic responsibility by 'those set in authority over their fellow human beings' and urges specific training in this regard for a range of such professions.[14]

The NCC guidelines also betray an occasional civic–republican influence. For example, the simple statement that 'education for citizenship . . . encourages [pupils] to develop . . . a desire to participate in events in the world about them'[15] could be construed in this manner. But perhaps more telling is the general requirement that citizenship education must be started at the very beginning of school life. A civic mode of thinking and behaving is to be instilled as early as Key Stage 1. Moreover, the holistic approach to the theme – its infusion into the various subjects of the curriculum, its characterization of the school ethos, the importance attached to relations with the local community – all this smacks more of the civic–republican than liberal–individualistic style of citizenship.

Because the Speaker's Commission failed to conduct a full theoretical analysis we have neither a consideration of the strand in liberal thinking concerning non-involvement, at one end of the commitment spectrum, nor, at the other, the republican view that civic participation is a *sine qua non* for the full moral development of the individual. Similarly, there is no consideration of the liberal case for citizenship as a hedge against government abuse of power, nor of the republican conception of citizenship as political (as opposed to social) participation. The omission of each of these facets perhaps over-simplifies the teacher's task and could distort the messages conveyed in the schools.

There is a similar failure to come to terms with the problems associated with rendering state and multiple citizenship compatible. Some of the best pages in *Encouraging Citizenship* are Piers Gardner's appendix, 'What Lawyers mean by Citizenship'. In this he distinguishes between traditional 'nationality citizenship' and what he calls 'new citizenship'. By the latter term he means a more sophisticated version of what has been called in this paper 'multiple citizenship' – more sophisticated because he handles all the complex nuances of British and international law. There are some echoes of Gardner's exposition in simplified form in the body of the report. Most explicitly there is the statement that:

> A British citizen is a member of a legally defined national community, and should, in consequence of a long period of evolution, enjoy civil, political and social entitlements and duties that go with the status. Secondly, such entitlements and duties extend beyond national frontiers as the result of national membership of broader groups – for example, the European Community. Finally, we can speak of a world community, with rights in international law in the post-war period.[16]

The basic truth that a Briton is simultaneously a member of a national, a European and a world community is mentioned on several pages of the NCC publication. It is reinforced by the use throughout of the logo for the component on 'Community': this is a representation of the UK, European Community and UN flags.

And yet the greatest emphasis in both documents, as one would expect, is placed upon national citizenship. This is particularly noticeable in Section III of the report of the Speaker's Commission, 'Encouraging Citizenship'. The stress on the local community voluntary work of the 'active citizen' must inevitably lead to a neglect of the broader context. A similar general message is projected by the NCC document.

Indeed, citizenship beyond the nation-state appears from these two publications to mean little more than a knowledge of the sundry human-rights documents. Nowhere are we alerted to the problems associated with multiple identities and loyalties. Nor, in particular, is there any discussion concerning the steady firming up of European citizenship and its implications for teaching.

CONCLUSION

Although tensions may be perceived between various interpretations and expressions of the basic concept of citizenship, these different emphases are not necessarily utterly incompatible. The tensions may be resolved – and should be for the sake of coherent teaching.

It is quite unreasonable to expect every individual to behave like the idealized politically virtuous Roman. And no teacher engaged in citizenship education should envisage his or her class as serried ranks of little Ciceros and Senecas. But the teacher charged with this area of work does have two responsibilities – both to each child and to the communities of which that child is a member. One is to ensure that all the younger generation develop a basic commitment to the positive values of those communities. The second is to provide sufficient knowledge and experience for those who are so inclined to be able to pursue the fullest civic life possible.

Whether that full civic life is shaped in the liberal or republican mould again must be the individual's choice. But two observations may help to place this choice in perspective. The first is that the dichotomy which some commentators have emphasized has perhaps been exaggerated. Both traditions recognize the basic range of citizenly attributes: the reciprocal rights and duties, identity and loyalty, and good civic behaviour. The second is that, whereas the republican style demands greater altruism on the part of the citizen, it should be remembered that that tradition was forged in circumstances in which the citizen body was smaller than today. It must be conceded that a full measure of civic zeal can perhaps only be realistically expected of an elite.

Finally, on the matter of national and multiple citizenship, some form of multiple identity is becoming increasingly necessary and increasingly easy, in some societies, for individuals to feel.[17] What is needed is a clarification and simplification of the law, both municipal and international, so that the individual can easily understand the rights and duties that attach to each role.

Analysis is the academic vice. In the matter of citizenship we must try to ensure that synthesis becomes the pedagogical virtue.

NOTES

1. David's painting *Brutus* (1789) shows the power of civic–republicanism in France at the time, as does his celebration of devoted military service, *The Oath of the Horatii* (1785).
2. M C Havens, 'Citizenship', *Encyclopaedia Americana*, p. 742.
3. See D Heater, 'Education for European Citizenship', *Westminster Studies in Education* (forthcoming).

4. Speaker's Commission on Citizenship (1990) *Encouraging Citizenship*, London: HMSO.
5. National Curriculum Council (1990) *Curriculum Guidance 8: Education for Citizenship*, York: NCC.
6. *Encouraging Citizenship*, p. 42.
7. *Encouraging Citizenship*, p. 102.
8. *Education for Citizenship*, Foreword.
9. *Encouraging Citizenship*, p. 103.
10. *Encouraging Citizenship*, p. 103.
11. *Education for Citizenship*, p. 6.
12. *Education for Citizenship*, p. 6.
13. *Encouraging Citizenship*, p. 39.
14. *Encouraging Citizenship*, p. 41.
15. *Education for Citizenship*, p. 6.
16. *Encouraging Citizenship*, p. 12.
17. See A D Smith (1991) *National Identity*, Harmondsworth: Penguin.

REFERENCES

Boyd, W (ed.) (1956) *Émile for Today: The Émile of Jean-Jacques Rousseau*, London: Heinemann.
Brennan, T (1981) *Political Education and Democracy*, Cambridge: Cambridge University Press.
Crick, B (n.d.) *Political Theory and Practice*, London: Allen Lane.
Curtis, S J and Boultwood, M E A (1956) *A Short History of Educational Ideas*, London: University Tutorial Press, 2nd edition.
Forsyth, M (1981) *Unions of States*, Leicester: Leicester University Press.
Forsyth, M G, Keens-Sopee, H M A and Savigear, P (eds.) (1970) *The Theory of International Relations*, London: Allen and Unwin.
Macfarlane, L J (1970) *Modern Political Theory*, London: Nelson.
Marshall, T H (1950) *Citizenship and Social Class*, Cambridge: Cambridge University Press.
O'Gorman, F (1986) *British Conservatism: Conservative Thought from Burke to Thatcher*, London: Longman.
Oldfield, A (1990) 'Citizenship: An unnatural practice?', *Political Quarterly*, vol. 61.
Oldfield, A (1990), *Citizenship and Community: Civic Republicanism and the Modern World*, London: Routledge.
Speaker's Commission on Citizenship (1990) *Encouraging Citizenship*, London: HMSO.
Rousseau, J-J (1969) *Oeuvres Complêtes* IV, Dijon: Gallimard.

Chapter 2

Citizenship and Minorities

Sally Tomlinson

The ultimate question is always about belonging.
M Ignatieff, 1991

INTRODUCTION

In the modern world the issue of *who belongs* to particular nation-states, with citizenship entitlements, is of crucial importance. Debates about citizenship are not academic. People are prepared to die in pursuit of their claims to be recognized as citizens of particular territories as well as for recognition of their ethnic or cultural identity. National majorities are prepared to use all strategies – including violence – to exclude minority groups from citizenship rights.

As post-war migration into Britain of minority groups variously perceived to be ethnically, racially or culturally different[1] has now virtually ended, and the incorporation of these groups as permanent citizens and settlers has begun, questions about what it means to be a citizen in the British nation, and to share a national identity and cultural heritage, have begun to be raised in a variety of forms. The question as to how far membership of a British national identity with full citizenship rights and obligations will be offered to non-white minorities is still very much an open one. Heater (1990) has suggested that 'citizenship in the Western liberal tradition presupposes that the citizens and the state are mutually respectful and supportive' (p. 97). This has never been a situation that racial and cultural minorities in Britain would recognize. Instead, minorities from former colonial countries, encouraged by the state to migrate to work in Britain, have faced a 40-year struggle to acquire and to exercise their political, civil and social citizenship rights. They have also faced a white majority seemingly determined to reject non-white groups as equal citizens within the British nation. The Committee of Enquiry chaired by Lord Swann (DES, 1985) envisaged Britain as a plural democracy in which the rights and obligations of all communities towards each other would be defined, protected and respected, with education playing a key role in the process. The reality in the 1990s is that the claims of non-white groups to be full citizens and part of the British nation are still suspect, and multicultural education is derided as left-wing ideology or conspiracy (Palmer, 1986; Lewis, 1988).

This chapter, then, is concerned with unresolved issues of citizenship. It examines the political resistance to the inclusion of minorities as equal citizens in Britain and notes the crisis of national identity that underpins this resistance, and the support for a 'nationalistic' rather than a multicultural education. The chapter concludes with some positive suggestions for a citizenship that recognizes ethnic and cultural differences.

A CHRONOLOGY OF EVENTS RELATING TO CITIZENSHIP AND MINORITIES

It is useful to begin with a chronology of events that are connected to issues of citizenship for racial and cultural minorities. Of note, over the 40 years covered by this chronology, is the preoccupation with the exclusion of migrants and minorities rather than with their citizenship potentialities, and the continued expression of prejudice and racism by some politicians, which have set the context for debate about the status of non-white minorities.

It should also be noted that by the 1970s Britain was unique in Europe, in that it had offered citizenship to former colonial subjects and had passed anti-discrimination laws. Read and Simpson (1992) have, however, commented that 'those with even the most remote knowledge of race relations in Britain know that both these "facts" are only worth mentioning in the most heavily qualified terms' (p. 30).

1948   S S *Empire Windrush* brings 492 immigrants from Jamaica to London.

1948   British Nationality Act distinguishes between citizens of the United Kingdom and Colonies and citizens of the independent Commonwealth.

1949   Attack by white working men on a hostel for black men in Deptford.

1952–56 Two private members' Bills to outlaw discrimination in public places not passed.

1958   White youths sentenced for attacking black people in Notting Hill, London.

1960   Number of immigrants from India, Pakistan and the Caribbean approximately 222,000.

1960   Birmingham Immigrant Control Association set up.

1961   Conservative Conference calls for immigration control.

1962   Commonwealth Immigration Act. Entry of migrants subject to holding of employment vouchers.

1964   Vouchers restricted to category A people with special skills and Category B for pre-arranged jobs.

1965   White paper on Commonwealth Immigration reduces the number of employment vouchers to 8,500. Department of Education circular 7/65 recommends that no school have over 30% immigrant children. First Race Relations Act passed: National Committee for Commonwealth Immigrants (NCCI) set up.

1966   Home Secretary Roy Jenkins posits a society based on 'cultural diversity and mutual tolerance' and expresses fear of consequences if a second generation is not given equal opportunity.

1967   Enoch Powell speaks and writes against entry of dependents of migrants and against the 'great influx of coloured immigrants from Kenya'.

1968   Home Secretary Callaghan introduces a Commonwealth Immigration Act that distinguishes between British citizens who are 'patrials' (have a parent or grandparent born in Britain) and those who are 'non-patrials'. Enoch Powell speaks of a 'nation heaping up its own funeral pyre' and sees 'the Tiber foaming with much blood' in a speech on immigration. Edward Heath drops Powell from the Shadow Cabinet but London dockers and Smithfield meat porters march to Westminster to support him. Eighty resolutions on immigration tabled at the Conservative Conference. Second Race Relations Act passed: NCCI superseded by the Community Relations Commission.

1969   Enoch Powell proposes a Ministry to deal with repatriation.

1970   UK Immigrants Advisory Service set up.

1971   New Immigration Act restricts the right of abode to 'patrials'. Others must obtain a work permit and register with the police. Census data indicate approximately 1,400,000 'non-white' people in Britain, half born in the country.

1972   Ugandan Asians (approximately 27,000) arrive, having been ejected by Idi Amin – 21,000 pass through special camps.

1973   Pakistan secedes from the Commonwealth, having lost East Pakistan, which becomes Bangladesh.

1974–77   Political and Economic Planning produces reports detailing the extent of discrimination in Britain against racial minorities, especially in housing, employment and the social services.

1974   Department of Education report on 'Educational Disadvantage and the Needs of Immigrants' – which are seen as synonymous.

1976   Third Race Relations Act: the Commission for Racial Equality is set up in place of the Community Relations Commission. William Whitelaw speaks on immigration and says that 'The British Empire has paid its debts'. He calls for major programmes in inner cities to 'defuse racial tensions'.

1977   Enoch Powell refers to 'enclaves of foreign lands' in British cities and envisages civil war. In Birmingham Stetchford the National Front candidate beats the Liberal into third place in a by-election. The non-white population is estimated at 3.3% of total population.

1979   Mrs Thatcher comments in a TV interview that many people in inner cities feel 'swamped' by alien cultures.

1980–86   Sporadic racial conflicts in major British cities. Government reacts with inner city programmes and projects and more policing.

1981   British Nationality Act (operative April 1983): approximately three million non-white British citizens are confirmed in their status. Approximately one million become third-country nationals (non-EC) with rights of residence in Britain but not abroad.

1982   During the Falklands War a *Sunday Telegraph* article (23/5/82) asserts that 'if the Falkland Islanders were British citizens with black or brown skins, spoke with strange accents or worshipped strange gods, it is doubtful whether the Royal Navy would be fighting for their liberation'.

1984   PSI study *Black and White Britain* documents continued racial discrimination and unequal rights for minorities.

1985   The Commission for Racial Equality publishes *Immigration Control Procedures*, noting that the process of bringing in families and acquiring citizenship rights was 'riddled with racist practice and prejudice'.

1986 Single European Act (operative December 1992), intended to remove internal frontier controls and lift restrictions on the rights of EC citizens to live and work anywhere in the EC. The one million UK third-country nationals fear they will not be able to travel to Europe. EC countries begin to express concern about immigration, refugees and asylum-seekers.

1986 Chris Patten, a Minister of State for Education, comments that 'in "white" areas there is a genuine and not dishonourable fear that British values and traditions will be put at risk if too much allowance is made for the cultural backgrounds of ethnic minorities'.

1987 Sir David Lane, first Chair of the CRE and a former Conservative MP, complains that 'in eight years as Prime Minister Mrs Thatcher has not made a single speech denouncing racialism and discrimination'.

1987 Four black MPs enter Parliament.

1988 The Education Reform Act is passed but does not mention race, ethnicity or multicultural education.

1989 A Foreign Office report suggests restricting immigration from Hong Kong to 'key professional and industrial personnel' when the Colony reverts to China in 1997.

1990 Norman Tebbitt proposes a 'cricket test': the loyalty to Britain of people of Asian origin should be judged by the cricket team they cheer for (*The Times* 21/4/90).

1990 The National Curriculum Council publishes *Education for Citizenship*, which includes half a page on 'a pluralist society', but suppresses a report it commissioned on multicultural education in schools.

1991 The High Court rules that parental choice of school overrides race-relations considerations. The court holds Cleveland County Council had been right to agree to a mother's request to move her child from a school with many Asian children.

1991 The Conservative Government publishes its *Citizen's Charter*. One mention is made of 'race': that 'services should be available regardless of race or sex'.

POLITICAL RESISTANCE

Any discussion of events relating to the inclusion of minorities as citizens in the UK has to take account of political and ideological resistance, which has characterized the post-war period. The claim of former colonial people to be accepted as British citizens has its roots in the British Empire, which was for some 400 years the economic and political base of the United Kingdom. It was at the point of the break-up of Empire that citizenship issues became acute, and the notion that any 'Imperial subject' had a freedom to migrate among British territories was challenged. The 1948 British Nationality Act was passed by a Labour Government as a consequence of Canadian legislation that established a Canadian citizenship. From 1948 two categories of British citizens were established, those of the UK and the Colonies (this category including non-white people with freedom to migrate to Britain) and citizens of the independent Commonwealth. Much of the tension arising from this Act was due to the fact that it allowed migration of 'new' Commonwealth non-white people, while ostensibly restricting the rights of settlers in the 'white' Commonwealth.

There is no doubt that the major political ideologies within which party politics is conducted in Britain have been, and still are, under severe strain concerning issues of immigration and race. Over the past 30 years *all* political parties have to some extent come to acquiesce in a process of political, legal and moral denigration of racially and culturally different groups. The post-war Conservative position originally revolved around an acceptance that all British citizens, of whatever colour or culture, had equal rights before the law. *Civis Britannicus sum* was a claim to legal rights, but it was also compatible with the idea that non-white citizens, like 'colonial natives', were destined for lower-skilled occupations and their children to lower-level education. Agitation for immigration control was resisted by Conservative governments in the 1950s; but in 1962, R A Butler, the father of the 1944 Education Act, introduced the first Act to control Commonwealth immigration. In the late 1960s Enoch Powell became a charismatic figure in British politics, by espousing immigration control and repatriation policies that had previously been the preserve of the National Front party. Although initially repudiated by his own party, Powell's views became steadily more respectable, and in 1979 Conservative electoral success was perhaps enhanced by Mrs Thatcher's expressed anxiety that 'alien cultures were swamping British values'. In the 1980s, inner-city riots, with their threats to law and order, have certainly been turned to electoral advantage. An article in *The Times* in November 1985 presented urban areas of high black settlement as 'criminal sanctuaries, largely controlled by young blacks so alienated from authority that any law-enforcing incursion can turn them into urban battlegrounds'. This article noted:

> Ministers increasingly view the criminal core who rule these areas as a new enemy within, who must be eliminated through forceful policing. If they achieve this end, it could prove a second Falklands factor in the run up to the next general election. (Hughes, 1985.)

In the event, a Conservative victory in the 1987 election did not need a 'Falklands factor', but it might be asked here: What kind of citizenship is possible in a society where young, black British-born citizens are stigmatized as an enemy whose defeat will equal a successful colonial war?

Socialist beliefs in the 'brotherhood of man' have also been under severe strain, however, and the Labour movement, in its struggle to right wrongs suffered by the working class, has always been well fortified by a dash of xenophobia. Over the past 25 years notions of universal human rights and the working-class struggle have often excluded ethnic minorities. A reading of the diaries of the late Richard Crossman, a Labour Minister in the 1960s, shows that, by 1965, the Labour Cabinet had accepted that showing sympathy for 'immigrants' was a vote-loser (Crossman, 1975) and it was James Callaghan who, as Home Secretary in 1968, introduced a second Commonwealth Immigration Act. There has been an uncomfortable acceptance by Labour politicians that support for minorities does not win political power in white areas. Trade unions have been dogged by demands for separate 'black sections', and even the Nationl Union of Teachers, at its 1986 Easter conference, was embarrassed to find black teachers demanding secession. Nevertheless, in 1987 the Labour Party did become a party with four black Members of Parliament, a fifth being added in a by-election in 1991. Also in 1991, the Conservative Party defended, against local opposition, its selection of a black barrister to contest the Cheltenham seat in the 1992 general election.

Liberal politics, which has provided a 20th-century base for social reforms, had by the 1960s become committed to the acquisition of welfare and citizenship rights for minorities. Roy Jenkins' much-quoted 1966 speech, extolling 'equal opportunity and cultural diversity in an atmosphere of mutual tolerance', came to embody liberal goals, and was very influential within an education system that has always prided itself on its liberal attitudes. The liberal position has manifested itself in commitment to a 'race-relations industry' of community, social and educational workers, all anxious to encourage racial justice via equal education opportunities. But this 'industry', unlike other areas of industry, has been increasingly derided by both right and left. Overall, meanwhile, there has been an escalation of the presentation of ethnic minority citizens and their children as scapegoats for economic ills, as responsible for the state of the inner cities, and for breakdowns in law and order. This has made it difficult for any politicians or public figures to take a lead in positive action to improve the social, educational and economic position of minorities and their children. Even the Archbishop of Canterbury's report on urban priority areas, which pointed to a 'growing number of young people, many of them black, excluded by poverty or powerlessness from sharing the common life of our nation', and criticizing the lack of political will to tackle the problem, was labelled first Marxist, then irrelevant (Archbishop of Canterbury's Commission on Urban Priority Areas, 1985).

The political climate over the post-war years has not, therefore, been conducive to the development of notions of citizenship for minorities that would include equal opportunities, acceptance and respect. Certainly we have never, in Britain, been in the quasi-liberal situation described by Gunnar Myrdal in his seminal study of race relations in America, published in 1944, that of an 'American dilemma' (Myrdal, 1944), in which the treatment of black people was acknowledged to conflict with the notion of free and fair competition in an open society. In Britain, evidence rather suggests that from the 1950s the one 'cause' that could unite all social classes, without any dilemma, has been hostility to groups perceived as racially or culturally different – inside or outside Britain.

A CRISIS OF NATIONAL IDENTITY

Explanations for the intensity of political and popular resistance to the acceptance of former colonial subjects as equal citizens of the United Kingdom must be grounded in the history of the British Empire, colonial expansion and imperialism. The consequences of rule over large numbers of non-white people led during the 19th century to a variety of rationalizations for economic and political exploitation. Victorian discussions of 'race' helped to develop a complex collection of pseudo-scientific theories portraying non-whites as everything from 'savage and bestial figures' to 'helpless beings in need of missionary protection' (Rich, 1986, p. 12). The liberal evangelical movement that had achieved the abolition of slavery gradually gave way to a more powerful racial hostility based on economic exploitation, and the incorporation of Darwin's ideas of biological hierarchies led to the development of social Darwinism and claims of a genetic white British superiority over non-white races. Lloyd (1984), an historian of Empire, wrote that by the 1860s British popular opinion regarded 'the Empire's black and brown subjects as natural inferiors'. The idea of a 'blood brotherhood' and 'white nations' was propagated by Victorian eugenicists (Murray, 1905), and the populist idea of 'our kith and kin' survived into the war of independence in Zimbabwe in the 1970s. At the high point of Empire the Anglo–Saxon 'race' was presented as the world's superior group: biologically, economically, politically, linguistically and culturally superior to colonized and non-Anglo–Saxon 'races'. The strength of Victorian beliefs in white racial and cultural superiority has persisted through the ending of colonialism, and still strongly influences the perception of 'who belongs' to the British nation and who does not. The white majority in Britain selectively holds on to remnants of Victorian beliefs in order to sustain a narrow, parochial and intolerant view of who should be included within the boundaries of a national identity.

Those who view the national identity from the point of view of the former colonized have pointed out that, as Britain completes a transition from imperial status and ruler of colonies to national status with a dwindling influence on world affairs and an uncertain 'European' future, there is something of a crisis of national identity.

Salman Rushdie wrote in 1982 that 'Britain is undergoing a critical phase of its post-colonial period, and this crisis is not simply economic or political – it is a crisis of the whole culture, of the society's whole sense of itself' (Rushdie, 1982). By 1992 this crisis was, if anything, more acute. The English, up to World War II, knew 'who they were'. They had an identity founded on the internal colonization of the Welsh, Irish and Scots and the external colonization of a quarter of the world. They had a ruling elite with the role of administering the Empire, middle-class businessmen extracting profits from colonies and a working class who could regard themselves as superior to all 'colonials'. This identity was shattered by the arrival of migrant labour from former colonial countries. After three decades of pretence that 'assimilation' would take place and the migrants become indistinguishable from the majority, official rhetoric had by the mid-1980s, at the latest, accepted that Britain did incorporate ethnic and cultural diversity.

However, contradictory tensions of acceptance and rejection do underpin any discussion as to how far minority groups who are regarded as racially or culturally different will be accepted as full British citizens and part of a 'British' nation. There is still strong popular resistance to the idea that Britain is a multiracial, multicultural society. The Swann Committee recognized this when they wrote that calls for a plural society were likely to be interpreted by some as 'seeking to undermine an ill-defined and nebulous concept of true Britishness' (DES, 1985, p. 7). Attempts by minority groups to claim equal citizenship and also to assert a separate cultural, religious, 'racial' or linguistic identity have often been met with suspicion or resentment. In some cases minority groups have had to resort to legal action to have their 'rights' as a cultural or racial group recognized – as for example, in the case of Dawkin v. Crown Supplies (1989), when it was decided that a Rastafarian cannot be refused employment because he is unwililng to cut off his dreadlocks.

There is, in Britain, still very little discussion as to what a democratic plural society might actually look like, how the national identity could be redefined, and what the values underpinning a modern multicultural society might be. Instead, as Hall (1988) has suggested, the white British are continuing to construct stereotyped images of inferior cultures and peoples, and attempting to sustain an identity built on a rejection of minority groups as equal citizens.

EDUCATION FOR EXCLUSIVE NATIONALISM

By the mid-1980s the education system was becoming increasingly important in determining the relations between the majority society and minorities. A halting and contested movement towards the development of multicultural and anti-racist education and the creation of a less ethnocentric curriculum had been in evidence for some 30 years (Tomlinson, 1983; Craft, 1986) and the publication of the Swann Report (DES, 1985) had marked a high point in official acceptance that education had a vital role to play in helping all young people to accept ethnic and cultural minorities as their equal fellow-citizens. However, in the climate described above, in which few public figures have been willing to take a lead in asserting that minorities are part of the national identity and where minorities have so often been used as scapegoats for social and economic ills, it was perhaps unsurprising that educational change in a multicultural direction was slow and resistance so intense.

During the 1980s an educational right wing took full advantage of popular insecurities and uncertainties about national identity, citizenship and the role of education in a multicultural society. Influential individuals and groups presented multicultural education as a dangerous ideology, and developed their own, which took the form of an exclusive educational nationalism. This nationalism was both a backlash against liberal ideas of cultural pluralism and an encouragement to the white majority to consider the demands made by minorities so unreasonable as to preclude them from claims to equal citizenship rights.

Educational nationalism depends on the myth that minorities have complete choice and full opportunity to be assimilated into the British way of life and British culture: 'The responsibility for the adaptations and adjustments involved in settling in a new country lies entirely with those who have come here to settle and raise families of their own free will' (Honeyford, 1982). Within this view, minorities must be blamed for their own intransigence if they fail to adapt and adjust.

Educational resistance towards making changes in a system designed for a white majority has, over the past 30 years, illustrated the hypocritical position suggested by Dench (1986). Thus minorities are urged that the most appropriate way for them to achieve equality of opportunity and acceptance into the nation is to give up adherence to their own culture, language, customs and values and regard themselves as British, adhering to British values. At the same time the white majority, including some pupils, parents and teachers, remain hostile to or suspicious of the actual presence as well as the cultures of minorities and deny them entry to the 'nation'. Assimilation or integration, although urged on minorities, is impossible in a society where the majority culture includes political and cultural beliefs in white superiority and condones racial discrimination and harassment. However, educational nationalists deny that there are barriers placed in the way of minorities to prevent them from achieving educational credentials and training, other than those they create for themselves by inertia, unreasonable demands, lack of fluency in English, or a desire to hold on to their own cultures.

Educational nationalism also depends on a mythologized British heritage and culture, which is assumed to be monolithic and shared by all white individuals with no divisions by class or gender. It is built around an opposition to curriculum change or innovation that would present the British heritage and culture in a different light. History, geography, literature, religious education and social studies are singled out as subjects to remain British-oriented, while world studies, peace studies, social and life skills, sociology and political education are considered to be irrelevant subjects that should be abandoned.

Educational nationalist views are clearly articulated in the publications of the conservative Hillgate Group (1987). This group is particularly concerned that the educational establishment has allowed the development of a multicultural curriculum that they consider works against 'the traditional values of Western society' (Hillgate, 1987, p. 3). They oppose the recommendations of the Swann Committee on the grounds that it 'engages our post-colonial guilt feelings and threatens to destroy altogether the basis of our national culture' (p. 4).

The development of educational nationalism has relied on its proponents attacking *all* supporters of cultural pluralism, curriculum change, educational policies for minorities, and all varieties of multicultural, anti-racist education as being politically motivated and likely to be subversive. Honeyford, the former Bradford head teacher whose views have been given wide media coverage, has during the 1980s helped to make resistance to pluralism and educational change for the majority both educationally and politically respectable. In articles in the *Salisbury Review* in 1983 and 1984 he suggested that those advocating change were likely to be left-wing agitators, and used derogatory stereotypes of minorities to suggest that educational demands by minorities were suspect. He linked those who supported multicultural or anti-racist education to 'a hard core of left-wing political extremists' (Honeyford, 1983) and suggested that 'much of the pressure for a multicultural curriculum comes from the vehement radical left and black organizations' (Honeyford, 1984). His articles, as Halstead has noted (1988), are, for someone who writes about 'British traditions of civilized discourse and good-natured tolerance', largely negative about minorities and contain a 'significant core of insulting statements'. Asians are portrayed as given to diatribes that reflect 'the hysterical political temperament of the Indian subcontinent' and West Indians are portrayed as lacking in educational ambition (Halstead, p. 69). In 1987 Honeyford called for a public referendum on multicultural education to check the 'powerful multicultural and anti-racist lobby supported by Swann'.

Supporters of educational nationalism have been particularly concerned to link multicultural and anti-racist activity (including the work of the Swann Committee) to left-wing politics, and to suggest that it is the imposition of an alien philosophy, which has no popular mandate, on a British nation that is being unfairly denigrated. Baroness Cox, who particularly influenced the 1988 Education Act towards a predominantly Christian orientation, has suggested that some anti-racist teaching materials are simply 'propaganda designed to undermine our society by dishonest intellectual tactics and promote disaffection and conflict' (Cox, 1986, p. 80). Pearce, a Monday Club member, has argued that the Swann Committee wished to impose a fundamental change in the national culture regardless of national opinion. To him the crucial question is whether an indigenous British culture will maintain its predominance, as 'the native British have a right to preserve their way of life and this must mean that it is their culture which predominates in school' (Pearce, 1986, p. 141). Pearce considers that pluralism has become a cover for left-wing ideas and that the Swann report is 'brazenly anti-democratic and illiberal' in advocating educational change for the majority.

Savery (1987), a Bristol teacher, adopted the political metaphor of 'the enemy within' to suggest that anti-racist educational activities are 'the instrument of a neocolonialist minority who seek domination over our domestic territories and who wish to destroy forever the culture that has grown and flourished there'. Then in 1988 Lewis, a leader-writer on the *Daily Mail*, misrepresented the conclusions of the Swann report: 'the materials taught in all subjects are to be in accordance with the values of a multiracial society and to the detriment of British patriotic pride' (Lewis, 1988, p. 142).

Opposition to multicultural or anti-racist education or a changed education for all has thus centred on an educational nationalism that seeks to defend the nation's 'culture' against supposed left-wing, black or minority attacks (Tomlinson, 1990).

The success of the educational nationalists can be judged by the virtual disappearance of issues concerning race, ethnicity and culture from the educational agenda since the passing of the 1988 Education Reform Act. During the passage of the Act an amendment put forward in the Lords that the first clause, which requires the national curriculum to 'prepare pupils for the opportunities, responsibilities and experiences of adult life', should continue 'in a multicultural, multiracial society' failed, and was withdrawn. The Act required that the daily act of collective workshop in schools be 'wholly or mainly of a broadly Christian character'. The reform of Section 11 grants – intended to assist the education of minorities – discouraged the use of the grant for multicultural activities or teaching minority languages (Home Office, 1990). A *Times Educational Supplement* editorial in June 1990 suggested that 'despite a rhetoric of commitment to multiculturalism and social equality, government philosophy is now frankly assimilationist rather than pluralist and there seems a definite intent to starve multicultural education of resources and let it wither on the vine' (TES, 1990, A.23).

CITIZENSHIP AND DIVERSITY

Given the popular and political resistance to minority cultures and the strengths of educational nationalism, what hope is there that minorities will eventually be accepted as equal citizens and avoid becoming what Dahrendorf has described as 'marginalized semi-citizens' (Dahrendorf, 1990)? On the basis of evidence it would appear that Britain, or more precisely England, is a nation-state resisting the idea that it is a multicultural society, incorporating a variety of ethnic communities, and is even reluctant to accept that it is part of an intercultural Europe and an interdependent world. The enduring belief in the assimilation of minorities has precluded the development of a politics of diversity, in which it could be recognized that allegiance to a variety of cultural, religious, class, or other groups should not exclude people from the acquisition and exercise of full political, social and civil rights and obligations. The prevailing view is still that any group who carry claims for diversity too far should forfeit their citizenship rights.

It is important that a national identity be developed in which diversity does not preclude full citizenship. Parekh (1990) has suggested a model for an integrated citizenship that recognizes cultural and ethnic diversity as valuable, not as problematic. His suggestions are as follows:

1. It should be recognized that cultural differences are valuable national assets, which widen the range of lifestyles open to all citizens and bring different traditions into a mutually beneficial dialogue.

2. It should be recognized that cultural differences are fragile and can be preserved only by preserving the ethnic communities.
3. It should be conceded that ethnic communities strengthen rather than threaten Britain's social cohesion, as minority cultures bring new talents, ideas, skills and forms of social organization.
4. It should be recognized that economic, social and moral problems can be solved only by creating responsible and self-disciplined communities. It would be absurd to destroy those communities that do exist.
5. Minorities should be accepted as part of British society established to help develop a national public culture. They should be included as full citizens, determining the kind of society Britain should become and their own place in it. (Parekh, 1990, Chapter 2.)

Any model of a society in which minority groups and their diverse cultures are accepted and respected will depend heavily on a proper multicultural education for citizenship. Despite the strengths of educational nationalism there is a movement within education that could be harnessed to such a goal. Citizenship, in a variety of forms, is now part of the educational agenda. The Speaker's Commission on Citizenship reported in 1990 at a conference attended by over 500 educationalists (Fogelman, 1991); the National Curriculum Council has identified 'Education for Citizenship' as one of five cross-curricular themes (NCC, 1990); and in Wales a cross-curricular theme of 'community understanding' addresses issues of citizenship and cultural diversity.

The National Curriculum Council guidance includes a short section on 'A Pluralist Society', which notes that:

A democratic society is based on shared values, and a variety of cultures and lifestyles can be maintained within the framework of its laws. This component helps pupils to appreciate that all citizens can and must be equal. It increases awareness and works towards resolving some of the tensions and conflicts that occur between groups that perceive each other to be socially, racially, ethnically or culturally different. (NCC, 1990, p. 6.)

CONCLUSION

This chapter has been concerned with one of the major unresolved issues of citizenship in Britain – that of the incorporation of racial, ethnic and cultural minorities as equal citizens within the parameters of a British national identity. The chapter has provided a good deal of evidence that indicates that, over the past 40 years, leading politicians and other influential figures in the society have been preoccupied with the exclusion of minorities and the denigration of their cultures rather than with their citizenship potentialities and prospects.

It has been suggested that a crisis of national identity underpins reluctance to accept minorities as full and equal citizens and that the white British are still attempting to sustain an identity created primarily in late Victorian times, in which nonwhite minorities are excluded from full acceptance as part of the British nation. An educational nationalism that resists changing an educational system designed for a white majority hinders the process of creating a society in which cultural diversity is respected and minorities, as equal citizens, have an equal voice in determining the kind of society they wish to live in. Nevertheless, it is possible to develop models for an integrated citizenship that recognizes and respects cultural and ethnic diversity.

NOTES

1. This chapter does not debate what an ethnic, racial or cultural group 'is'. The reader is referred to Rex (1986), who makes the point that physical or cultural characteristics do not determine membership of a group. It is the behaviour and attitudes of others that determine whether a group is described as ethnic, racial or cultural.
2. Reactions to the setting up of a Muslim 'parliament' in 1992 included suggestions that those who supported Islamic separatist movements should lose their citizenship rights.

REFERENCES

Archbishop of Canterbury's Commission on Urban Priority Areas (1985) *A Call for Action*, London: Church House Publishing.

Cox, C (1986) 'From Auschwitz – Yesterday's Racism – to GCHQ, In: Palmer, F (ed.) *Anti-racism: an Assault on Education and Values*, Wiltshire: The Sherwood Press.

Craft, M (1986) 'Multicultural Education in the United Kingdom', In: Barks, J A and Lynch, J (eds) *Multicultural Education in Western Societies*, London: Holt, Rhinehart and Winston.

Crossman, R (1975) *Diaries of a Cabinet Minister*, London: Hamish Hamilton.

Dahrendorf, Sir R (1990) 'Decade of the Citizen', *The Guardian*, 1/6/90.

Dench, G (1986) *Minorities in an Open Society: Prisoners of Ambivalence*, London: Routledge.

Department of Education and Science (1985) *Education for All* [The Swann Report], London: HMSO.

Fogelman, K (1991) *Citizenship in Schools*, London: David Fulton.

Hall, S (1988) Invited lecture at the University of Lancaster. 17/5/88.

Halstead, M (1988) *Education, Justice and Cultural Diversity*, Lewes: Falmer Press.

Heater, D (1990) *Citizenship: The Civic Ideal in World History, Politics and Education*, London: Longman.

Hillgate Group (1987) *The Reform of British Education*, London: The Claridge Press.

Home Office (1990) *Section 11 of the Local Government Act: Grant Administration Proposals*. London: Home Office.

Honeyford, R (1982) 'Multiracial Myths?', *The Times Educational Supplement* 19/11/82.

Honeyford, R (1983) 'Multi-ethnic Intolerance', *Salisbury Review* 4, June, 12–13.

Honeyford, R (1984) 'Education and Race: An Alternative View, *Salisbury Review* 6, December, 30–32.

Hughes, C (1985) 'Keeping the lid on the inner cities', *The Times* 19/11/85.

Ignatieff, M (1991) 'The New Jigsaw of History', *Observer* 29/12/91.

Lewis, R (1988) *Anti-Racism: A Mania Exposed*, London: Quartet Books.

Lloyd, T O (1984) *The British Empire 1558–1983*, Oxford: Oxford University Press.

Murray, S (1905) *The Peace of the Anglo-Saxons*, London: Watts and Co.

Myrdal, G (1944) *The American Dilemma*, New York: Harper and Row.

National Curriculum Council (1990) *Curriculum Guidance 8: Education for Citizenship*, York: NCC.

Palmer, F (ed.) (1986) *Anti-racism: An Assault on Education and Values*, Wiltshire: Sherwood Press.

Parekh, B (1990) 'British Citizenship and Cultural Difference' In: Andrews, G (ed.) *Citizenship*, London: Lawrence and Wishart.

Pearce, S (1986) 'Swann and the Spirit of the Age', In: Palmer, F (ed.) *Anti-racism: An Assault on Education and Values*, Wiltshire: Sherwood Press.

Read, M and Simpson, A (1992) *Against a Rising Tide: Racism, Europe and 1992*, Nottingham: Nottingham Racial Equality Council.

Rex, J (1986) *Race and Ethnicity*, Milton Keynes: Open University Press.

Rich, P (1986) *Race and Empire in British Politics*, Cambridge: Cambridge University Press.

Rushdie, S (1982) 'The New Empire within Britain', *New Society* 9/12/82.

Savery, J (1987) 'Strictly Anti-Racist on Fantasy Island', *Salisbury Review* 5, 3, 4–6.

The Times (1990) 'Tebbit Defends Comments on Asians'. 21/4/90.

The Times Educational Supplement (1990) Editorial. June 1990.

Tomlinson, S (1983) *Ethnic Minorities in British Schools: a Review of the Literature 1960–82*, London: Heinemann.

Tomlinson, S (1990) *Multicultural Education in White Schools*, London: Batsford.

Chapter 3

The Citizen and the Law – Teaching about the Rights and Duties of Citizenship

Don Rowe

Citizenship has many facets and education for citizenship many more. In this chapter I intend to look at some of the issues raised by teaching young people about the rights and duties of citizenship and about the law through which these are mediated. By definition, citizenship represents a relationship between the individual and one or more state communities. That relationship is formally defined by means of a complex network of legal rules establishing both the rights and the duties that come with membership of that community. However, the nature of the relationship is much more complex than this simple definition would suggest and therefore educating for citizenship must go far beyond the mere transmission of citizenship knowledge.

In considering the nature of citizenship learning, I believe it is helpful to regard formal citizenship as just one of many kinds of group or community membership that people experience. Because learning acquired in one community is at least partly transferable to the others we must identify characteristics that these different communities have in common and consider their relevance to the question of membership. Among these commonalities we should include leadership, power, a rule-frame, decision-making procedures, shared and unshared values. All communities depend for coherence on a degree of social bonding.

Further, the strength of affiliation or bonding to each community has a critical effect on the motivation of members to accept or reject the duties of membership. Individual members are more likely to feel strongly bonded to communities where emotional or affective ties are reinforced by a sense of shared aims and values. I would identify five types of community as follows.

The family community

The family acts as a mini-society, having a power structure, rules, a system of punishment and rewards, a framework of values (implicit and explicit), and very strong emotional ties. The family is probably the crucible of citizenship learning.

The affiliative community

Affiliative communities are those that an individual may choose to identify with and may include peer groups, professional bodies, interest groups and religious groups. Organizationally they have formal or informal structures similar to other communities. A marked feature of the affiliative community is the extent to which individual members will identify with the group. Thus social bonding may be very strong.

The school community

Schools are highly complex communities, differing from affiliative communities because of their compulsory nature. School communities have much in common with state communities in the way they function and the nature of the demands they make on their members. They have value systems linked to their purpose and role, power structures and rules backed up by a justice system. In addition, they have 'citizens' or 'subjects' exhibiting different degrees of loyalty to the community. School communities are threatened by disaffected elements, which cannot simply be discarded. They may, therefore, take steps to reduce alienation by engendering a sense of community pride, of shared purpose and values, and by encouraging a feeling that all their members matter.

The state community

These can exist at local, national and international level and are formally defined through legislation setting out the rights and duties of their citizens. Membership is not usually voluntary for most citizens. Often individuals may feel less of a sense of loyalty to these state communities because of their mandatory nature, their remoteness or, perhaps, because of their perceived faults. Identification by citizens with the state may be very strong, particularly in the face of external threat, but where some citizens feel themselves to have less access than others to the benefits conferred by the state, they are likely to feel less of a sense of shared identity and social bonding will be weakened. State communities have often felt it essential to promote a sense of belonging through, for example, the use of patriotic devices. Schools are often seen as crucial to the task of developing a sense of identity with the state.

The world community

The notion of world citizenship is more complex than, and different in nature from, state citizenship. It appears to combine elements akin to membership of the state and the family. Through the United Nations and international agreements and treaties we can identify state-like structures embodying laws, sanctions, rights and duties. For individuals membership of the world 'state' comes through the affiliation of the nation-state to international agreements. In this sense, membership of the world community is inescapable, as is membership of the state. In a more personal sense, one is born into membership of the world community as one is born into a family. A sense of common humanity is for many a profoundly unifying force, which may gain added meaning as all members of the world become increasingly interdependent. Threats to global survival can emphasize this sense of oneness, as do beliefs in universal human rights. However, in practice these ideas appear to be too remote to have real meaning for perhaps the majority of people and they remain obscured by more immediate cultural differences and economic interests.

This analysis serves to highlight a number of aspects of citizenship that are salient to our present discussion. Firstly, citizenship learning is highly complex. It involves both cognitive and experiential learning, which is transferable between communities. This means that for younger children, ideas and beliefs about their own 'citizenship' tend to be more strongly influenced by communities near at hand and these ideas become transferred to the wider community (Torney, 1971). Therefore the family and the school are enormously important arenas of citizenship learning. In addition, the individual's sense of self-esteem and respect for others, which develop within these communities, have a significant influence on attitudes towards the community as a whole. Emler and Reicher (1987), for example, found that the anti-authority attitudes of some adolescents tended to be uniform across all the authority figures they encountered. Thus a young person whose experience of the family or the school has been an alienating one is unlikely to view the state community much differently.

Secondly, people's everyday experiences are of belonging to a multiplicity of communities that in practice frequently give rise to conflicting demands. The relative strength with which the individual is bonded to each community will influence how such conflicts are resolved. For example, it appears to be an almost inviolable rule that loyalty to members of one's family overrides loyalty to the state. Similar conflicts have led journalists, for example, to defy the law over disclosure of their sources and Sikhs to behave similarly over the wearing of crash helmets. This type of conflict helps to explain why for many young people, membership of the peer-group community is of greater personal significance than obedience to the law.

Talk of participative citizenship (for example, in *Curriculum Guidance 8* (National Curriculum Council, 1990)) often rests on the assumption that citizens share a commitment to the common good. But this is not always the case. On the other hand, many citizens voluntarily serve the community in ways that far exceed the legal duties of citizenship. Not all acts of personal or social kindness are acts of citizenship *per se*.

Some models of citizenship emphasize its rights and responsibilities (*status*) while others stress the affective element and, in particular, that citizenship involves caring for the welfare of the community and/or its members. This is often couched in the language of *service*. Writings about citizenship often contain these two components, though not necessarily always clearly differentiated (Porter, 1991). It is suggested here that both elements are important to a healthy community but that they must be separately understood. Different models of citizenship can be identified using the two components of status and service as in Figure 3.1.

Figure 3.1   *The components of status and service, used in analysing models of citizenship*

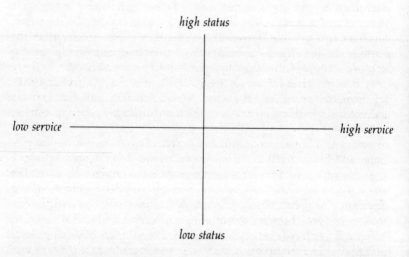

A philosophy of citizenship *high on service* and *low on status* dominated much of the thinking about citizenship in the early years of the century. This was undoubtedly influenced by the Christian ideal of love but its weakness was that it placed relatively little emphasis on the legal rights of citizens and on the inequalities in society that resulted in uneven enjoyment of full citizenship status. This view relegates pro-social acts to the beneficence of individuals and thus to chance. This is to undermine the concept of *right* or *entitlement* and to devalue the role of the state in ensuring that citizens receive their rights.

A philosophy of citizenship *high on status* and *low on service* emphasizes the role of the state in ensuring that the rights and freedoms of citizenship are maintained. But a society in which the minimum standards of the law were upheld would be an impoverished one. For example, while the law can legislate against racial discrimination it is unable to compel people to set aside their prejudices. This view is a passive one, which emphasizes the role of the state in the delivery of people's entitlements and places less importance on the role of the voluntary sector. It also ignores the vital importance of the citizens' personal commitment towards safeguarding or improving the status of citizens generally.

A view of citizenship *high on status* and *high on service* emphasizes the close relationship between being (and feeling) a valued member of the community and developing positive attitudes towards participative citizenship. It points up the necessity to develop the affective side of citizenship education in parallel with the development of understanding. This model of citizenship is supported by a great deal of psychological evidence that suggests that individuals with a high self-esteem are more likely to exhibit pro-social attitudes. This view would therefore emphasize that an appreciation that one has rights is necessarily prior to respecting similar rights in others. One of the lessons of history is that much of the energy needed to change the legal entitlements of citizenship comes from the voluntary commitment of those who believe the status quo to be inadequate or unjust.

A view of citizenship *low in status* and *low in service* would characterize an alienated or antisocial stance. Where social bonding is low and individuals feel themselves disenfranchised from the rights or benefits of a society, there may well be a feeling that the only option is to look after one's own interests. For many people in this category the problem may not be so much that they wilfully disregard the rights of others as that they are unable to recognize that such rights or needs exist. This emphasizes the importance of an educational model of citizenship that develops positive attitudes and moral awarenesss combined with a clear understanding of the nature of one's rights and duties. But given the complexity of the task, how should we set about teaching young people about their legal rights and duties? It is to this problem that I now wish to turn.

For a variety of social and cultural reasons, there is no long-standing tradition in the UK of teaching pupils about the law or the rights and duties of citizenship and therefore the recent guidance contained in *Curriculum Guidance 8: Education for Citizenship* represents a significant challenge. This document includes among its components 'The Citizen and the Law', 'Being a Citizen (Rights and Responsibilities)' and 'Democracy in Action'. These three elements are closely interlinked and are vital to the provision of a broad and balanced citizenship programme.

Awareness of the failure of the curriculum to address these particular areas has been steadily growing for a number of years (for a useful review of the main trends in this century, see Brown, 1991). In the 1970s, the raising of the school-leaving age to 16 and the lowering of the age of voting to 18 brought more sharply into focus the role of schools in preparing young people for participation and responsibility and to enable them to understand many of the basic elements of the social structure. The increasing urgency of the need was expressed unusually strongly by Her Majesty's Inspectorate in *Curriculum 11–16* (1977):

> Insofar as pupils may marry at 16, vote at 18 and become involved in legal responsibilities, what has the curriculum – the schools' deliberate educational policy – done to help them in these matters of fundamental importance to adult life? More than this, even though it may sound somewhat grandly put, pupils are members of a complicated civilization and culture, and it is reasonable to argue that they have nothing less than a right to be introduced to a selection of its essential elements.

Added to these concerns were others regarding rising juvenile crime and the apparently growing rift in some quarters between the police and young people, which at its most extreme expressed itself in street riots. The riots of the summer of 1981 were particularly violent and widespread and led to an enquiry headed by Lord Scarman (1981). The enquiry concluded that the police should redouble their efforts to build bridges between themselves and young people. This, it was hoped, would result in a generation of young people better informed about, and more supportive of, the police and less likely to engage in juvenile crime. At school level, the Scarman Report resulted in a significant increase in the joint development of police/schools programmes. Several official reports during the 1980s (for example, ACPO/SEO 1986, HMI 1982 and 1989) endorsed the value of cooperation between teachers and the police and attempted to define more clearly the educational aims of such programmes. Despite the increased activity, however, much of the work was still relatively unsophisticated, with little attempt to relate the origins of antisocial attitudes to what is known from research about the growth of moral maturity and social responsibility (Rowe, 1990, 1992).

In fairness, it must be said that those who wished to develop courses on the law and crime had little to draw on. Until the early 1980s there had been virtually no developments in this field in the UK, except where the treatment was of a sociological kind, focusing on penology, criminology and law-and-order issues. This still left the area of 'citizen's law' largely uncharted (with the exception of some elements of consumer law). However, a tide of opinion was running in favour of a core social curriculum and an approach from the Law Society to fund a curriculum development project was welcomed by the School Curriculum Development Committee (SCDC). Taking its inspiration from work undertaken in the United States (see, for example, American Bar Association, 1976, and Gerlach and Lamprecht, 1975), the Law Society had thoroughly researched the field before committing major funds to this project. In a survey commissioned from MORI (1980) there was found to be considerable interest among teachers in introducing young people to the law. The survey confirmed that there was an almost complete lack of materials for use outside existing A- and O-level law courses (CSE law being virtually nonexistent). This was clear evidence, if it were needed, that schools had failed to challenge the received view that the law was a subject suitable only for an academic elite. These courses continued to reflect the legal-training model dominant in the universities and were not designed to address the needs of ordinary citizens.

There is, in fact, considerable evidence that lack of legal awareness among the population at large is a significant problem. As Barbalet (1988) notes, the question of citizenship is not simply bound up with the extent of the relevant rights and duties; it is as much to do with citizens' capacity to make use of them. Barriers to citizenship include ignorance of the law and lack of self-confidence and skill to discover and use it effectively. For example, in *Ordinary Justice* the National Consumer Council (1989) concluded:

> We have found that, in practice, most people forego their rights. Individual consumers [of the legal system] start at a disadvantage because they meet the legal system only rarely and have a limited understanding of how it works and limited resources in terms of money, time and energy. . . . Most people do not even consider going to law.

In its report on the future of the legal profession the Marre Committee (1988) noted that, for example, only 50% of those entitled to claim family credit actually did so, and that few people were able to claim their entitlements in situations such as unlawful discrimination, unfair dismissal or industrial injury. Reasons for this included ignorance of the existence of such rights and of free or inexpensive channels to pursue them. There was also evidence that people harboured exaggerated fears of becoming entangled in the legal system, even where there was a simple remedy available.

Younger people also encounter situations in which knowledge of their rights and duties would be beneficial – for example, in consumer, family, discrimination and employment law. Because of their age and inexperience young people are particularly prone to be exploited and victimized. Vorhaus (1984) found the majority of upper-secondary pupils stunningly ignorant of the law, even on such matters as to whom to turn for reliable help and advice.

Ignorance of the rights and responsibilities of citizenship can easily perpetuate injustice and foster an unhappy fatalism on the part of the disadvantaged. As society becomes structurally more complex, culturally more diverse and subject to more and more legislation, there exists the growing danger that citizens will see the law and the legal framework as increasingly remote and irrelevant to their daily lives. The dangers of this process for a democratic society cannot be overemphasized. Apathy, indifference and alienation are among the likely products of a system where the divide between the people and those who make, administer and enforce the law grows ever wider.

However, the task of introducing young people to the law is not a simple one. As a subject, the law can be highly complex and intellectually demanding, raising quite difficult problems in terms of content and level. It is also necessary to develop an appropriate balance between knowledge, skills and attitudes and to adopt the appropriate methodology to deliver these by means of an integrated approach. Bearing in mind that its purpose is to meet the real needs of citizens, I suggest we describe it as a *legal competence* model, to distinguish it from the kind of legal training one would expect from a more traditional course.

Legal competence, I suggest, must involve the following elements:

- Awareness of *the nature of law:* that, for example, it conveys rights that are balanced by responsibilities, and that it permeates many aspects of daily life. At its most basic this would at least raise the awareness of citizens to a point at which they are able to seek out appropriate help and advice rather than act (or fail to act) in legal ignorance.
- Understanding key elements of *the legal system*, including the differences between civil and criminal law, the nature of the justice system and the role of the police.
- Understanding how the law is made and changed, the nature of *the democratic processes*, and how individuals can promote social change.
- Being aware that laws are based upon *values and beliefs*, which may not be shared by all citizens. In particular, legal awareness should encourage an understanding that law is not always synonymous with justice.
- The *skills* to know when and how to discover the law, to seek appropriate help and advice and to act on it.
- The development of *attitudes* of respect for the rule of law and the rights of others.

The materials developed by the Law in Education Projects (1989 and 1993) have been based on this model of legal competence. During the trials of the Key Stage 4 materials, teachers were asked to evaluate this approach (Rowe, 1987). The response from over 50 teachers, most of them nonspecialists, was very positive. Some teachers saw the materials as introducing an element essential to the preparation of pupils for adult life:

> It allows pupils to see that the law can be used by them and not merely against them. . . . Pupils have a right to know how they are affected by the law in a passive sense and, perhaps more importantly, how they can empower themselves and actively enlist the help of the law.

Other teachers recognized the social value of helping future citizens understand the nature of the responsibilities they will face and of developing appropriate skills and attitudes:

> It poses them real-life situations that they are able to identify with, and the tasks provide opportunities to explore solutions. Above all, it helps foster positive attitudes to social responsibility. . . . As education is encouraged to be relevant, an awareness of the laws which govern us all is crucial if young people are to assume their social duties.

Some teachers found that the law provided a useful basis for the discussion of ethical issues that might otherwise lack structure. Particularly where cultural and personal values differ within a group, public policy provides a clear frame of reference. The law, after all, is the one code of conduct binding on all citizens, from whatever cultural background. One teacher, after discussing family law with a group not normally keen to discuss such issues, commented:

> The discussions as to how far the law should interfere or impose on family relationships were particularly useful. Protection of individuals and public policy were particularly discussed.

Pupils, also, were asked for their responses to the law modules they had undertaken. In particular, they were asked to indicate levels of interest and enjoyment and the extent to which they felt such knowledge was worthwhile. Well over three-quarters (82%) of the sample of 167 students said they had enjoyed the course, while 99% (165 students) expressed the view that knowing about the law was of value. Among the most frequently quoted reasons was that it was 'useful to know' or 'helpful'.

The response of teachers to the Law in Education (14–16) Project indicated that here was a curriculum area the potential of which was only just beginning to be explored. In order to ensure the continuation and extension of the work, The Citizenship Foundation was established in 1989, with the Law Project team forming the nucleus of the Foundation's staff. As a result of new negotiations between the Citizenship Foundation and the National Curriculum Council, funding was agreed for a new project to develop materials supporting the law-related citizenship curriculum of Key Stage 3. These materials were developed using a model similar to that used in the earlier project. An additional aid to planning for continuity and progression was the identification of a number of key citizenship concepts. I suggest that these concepts should be regarded as essential to the citizenship curriculum at *all* key stages. These are as follows:

- justice and fairness
- rights and responsibilities
- laws and rules
- power and authority
- democracy
- community
- conflict and cooperation
- diversity and interdependence
- freedom and constraint

These key concepts provide a guide to the core of what educating for citizenship is all about. Quite clearly, the list goes beyond laws and rules, which are a central concern of this chapter. However, laws and rules arise out of the need to regulate interpersonal or public affairs and citizens should be able to develop laws or rules that are fair. The law can therefore provide an excellent framework for the discussion of citizenship issues of all kinds. Let us take the example of abortion. This can be studied from a number of discrete standpoints, including physical, cultural, moral and religious. None of these different perspectives need take account of any of the others, but in answering the question 'What should the law say?' pupils will need to address all these conflicting dimensions and, in effect, form a view about the most suitable resolution of the problem from the points of view of the public good. With younger pupils, discussion of rules can achieve a similar purpose, the difference between laws and rules being more of context than principle.

Concept-based approaches are not always popular. They leave much to the teacher by way of planning and implementation, and teachers often incline, in practice, towards knowledge-based curricula. But knowledge is secondary to understanding and, without a clear idea of the governing concepts, course construction can lack direction and focus. A further advantage of using concepts as an organizing framework lies in the fact that, even where departments may offer little in the way of citizenship knowledge, they can nonetheless be seen to contribute to pupils' understanding of citizenship concepts. It is therefore possible to invite all departments of the school to reflect on how the experiences they offer are likely to influence pupils' view of, for example, justice, responsibility, rules/laws, power and authority (see, for example, an interesting experiment by Rodin [1992] with the maths and science departments in his school). Citizenship coordinators, undertaking curriculum audits, need to go beyond the topic-focused tick-sheet, however useful these might be as ice-breakers. The concepts provide the means by which the whole citizenship curriculum can be identified.

Using the same concepts to review the taught and the hidden curriculum, it becomes possible to consider the match between what is being taught in the classroom and the values that underlie the actual practice of the whole school community. The ethos of schools can have a considerable influence on pupils' developing social awareness. This was one of the central messages of the Elton Report on Discipline in Schools (1989): that where rules are clear, have a clearly understood rationale and are even-handedly enforced, pupils are more likely to develop positive attitudes towards authority and feel a sense of ownership, dignity and worth. In their report on secondary schools in 1988, HMI noted that a minority of schools had conspicuously failed to develop such rule frames. Through being either too authoritarian or too laissez-faire, schools were failing to provide clear and supportive frameworks for pupils and the negative effect of this on personal development, behaviour and relationships within the school was noted.

Schools, of course, are justice systems in their own right, and where teachers are the legislature and at the same time judge, jury and executioner the potential for injustice is heightened. In this respect, the international codes of human rights provide valuable guidance as to what rights should be accorded to pupils. Schools need seriously to examine how far their 'control agenda' is in conflict with the duty to accord pupils the same standard of justice and fair treatment that they are entitled to expect from the community. This is helpfully discussed in some detail by Cunningham (1991).

Effective citizenship can be achieved only as a result of the development of understanding, skills and attitudes in the long term. With education for citizenship, continuity and progression are vital, starting with the early years. The importance of the primary years in laying the foundations for positive and effective citizenship cannot be over-emphasized. Primary teachers may take the view that much of the explicit citizenship curriculum is more appropriate to the secondary school. This view has had a great deal of currency over the years. One of the strengths of *Curriculum Guidance 8*, however, is to emphasize the significance of planning for citizenship in the primary years. Here again, the key concepts are an important guide as to what aspects of early school life might be contributing towards citizenship learning. Even within Key Stage 1, where explicit discussion of citizenship issues may not be great, teachers will be aware that pupils are learning rapidly about rules and laws, justice and fairness and their own and other people's rights.

Of all the key concepts we have discussed, I suggest that the one most central to the citizenship curriculum is *justice*. Justice, as Rawls (1972) claimed, is the highest standard by which anything in the public domain may be judged. All the other key citizenship concepts may be reviewed in the light of the justice concept. In other words, citizens are entitled to criticize aspects of public life on the grounds of whether they are just or fair, and once something in the public domain, such as a law, can be shown to be just, it needs no further justification. If it is unjust, then it should not reasonably be sustained. Naturally, people differ in their view of what is just since the value base from which they make their judgements will differ. Justice is therefore a procedural rather than a substantive concept and should be based on respect for truth and basic human rights.

If this is accepted, then it follows that citizenship education must adopt a dynamic methodology, in which pupils are challenged to see their rights and responsibilities in their social and moral context and to develop a personal view about their fairness. The development of critical thinking is essential. Through learning methods that engage their thinking, pupils must be encouraged to develop the ability to reason both logically and morally. This is education for change rather than an uncritical induction into the duties of citizenship. As Dewey (1916) so tellingly put it:

> A society which not only changes but which has the ideal of such change as will improve it, will have different standards and methods of education from one which aims simply at the perpetuation of its own customs.

In a democratic society the citizen has a right, and arguably a moral duty, to exercise an element of control on those in power. Authority is delegated to governments by the people and the accountability of democratic governments demands that citizens exercise critical judgement and take a moral view. This is why schools should take every opportunity to encourage pupils of all ages to consider justice issues. These should be both planned and addressed as they arise within the daily life of the school.

Lawrence Kohlberg, working with Blatt (1975), found that classroom discussions of justice issues can be effective in encouraging progress towards greater moral maturity. Kohlberg (for example, 1984), following Piaget, claimed that this development takes place through qualitatively different stages. Young children require a comprehensive code of conduct to be established for them. They seem to be incapable of regulating their own behaviour. Thus they exhibit a *coerced* or 'rule-obeying' morality. Kohlberg claimed that the majority of people progress to a *conforming* or 'rule-maintaining' morality, in which their moral thinking becomes dominated by the need to maintain the social framework, including the rule of law. The most advanced moral stage may be called *critical* or 'rule-creating' – a morality in which a person's commitment to moral principles comes to be seen as more important than maintaining an unjust status quo for its own sake.

The above process is one of increasing internalization of rule-governed behaviour. This takes place partly as the result of natural cognitive development and partly through the stimulation of the moral environment. Many studies have demonstrated that pupils can be accelerated towards more sophisticated moral judgements through the discussion of moral problems, in which the ideas they hold are challenged by those of a slightly more 'advanced' stage. Furthermore, there appear to be significant links between the development of moral reasoning and the emergence of socially responsible behaviour. Arbuthnot and Gordon (1986), for example, investigated the effect of a programme of moral problem discussions with groups of behaviourally difficult pupils. After 16 to 20 weekly sessions, of about 45 minutes each, those in the treatment groups showed measurable gains both in their moral-reasoning scores and across a number of behavioural measures, compared with pupils in control groups.

In this way, I believe, it is possible to achieve a synthesis between the two models of citizenship we discussed at the beginning of the chapter. Citizenship both as legally defined *status* and as *service* relies ultimately on the citizen as a moral agent. The importance of emphasizing this moral view of citizenship is that, however just the framework of rules or laws, the quality of community life rests on the willingness of individuals to accept and exercise their rights and responsibilities fairly. This is the challenge at the core of education for citizenship.

This chapter has argued that law-related citizenship (in the wider sense) should be regarded as an essential element of every pupil's curriculum and that it should be consciously planned for at all stages of school life. Teaching about the citizen and the law, as recommended in *Curriculum Guidance 8*, represents a new and challenging enterprise, of which we are still undoubtedly in the early stages. Despite its novelty, I have tried to show how it integrates with, and brings more sharply into focus, many long-standing concerns relating to the role of the school in the development of personal and social responsibility. I have argued that it offers the possibility of relevant and rigorous learning opportunities for pupils of all ages and that it addresses many issues of fundamental importance, which for too long have gone by default.

REFERENCES

ACPO/SEO (1986) *Liaison between Police and Schools* (a joint report of the Association of Chief Police Officers and the Society of Education Officers).
American Bar Association (1976) *Law-related Education in America: Guidelines for the*

Future. Report of the ABA Special Committee on Youth Education for Citizenship.

Arbuthnot, J and Gordon, D A (1986) 'Behavioral and Cognitive Effects of a Moral Reasoning Development Intervention for High-Risk Behavior-Disordered Adolescents', *Journal of Consulting and Clinical Psychology*, 34, 208–216.

Barbalet, J M (1988) *Citizenship*, Milton Keynes: Open University Press.

Blatt, M and Kohlberg, L (1975) 'The Effects of Classroom Moral Discussion upon Children's Level of Moral Judgement', *Journal of Moral Education* 4, pp 129–163.

Brown, C (1991) 'Education for Citizenship: Old Wine in New Bottles?' *Citizenship* (the journal of The Citizenship Foundation) 1, 2.

Cunningham, J (1991) 'The Human Rights Secondary School' in *The Challenge of Human Rights Education*, Starkey (ed.) London: Cassell.

Dewey, J (1916) *Democracy and Education*, New York: Free Press.

Elton Report on Discipline in Schools (1989), London: HMSO Books.

Emler, N and Reicher, S (1987) 'Orientations to Institutional Authority in Adolescence', *Journal of Moral Education* 16, 2, 108–116.

Gerlach, R A and Lamprecht, L W (1975) *Teaching about the Law: A Guide to Secondary and Elementary School Instruction*, Cincinatti: Anderson Publishing Co.

Her Majesty's Inspectorate (1977) *Curriculum 11–16*, London: HMSO Books.

Her Majesty's Inspectorate (1983) *Police Liaison with the Education Service*, London: HMSO Books.

Her Majesty's Inspectorate (1988) *Secondary Schools*, London: HMSO Books.

Her Majesty's Inspectorate (1989) *Discipline in Schools*. Report of the Committee of Enquiry Chaired by Lord Elton, London: HMSO Books.

Her Majesty's Inspectorate (1989) *Our Policeman: Good Practice in Police/School Liaison*, London: HMSO Books.

Law in Education (11–14) Project (forthcoming) *Living with the Law: Citizenship for Key Stage 3*, vols 1–3. Rowe, D and Thorpe, T (eds), London: Hodder and Stoughton.

Law in Education (14–16) Project (1989) *Understand the Law*, vols 1–4. Rowe, D and Thorpe, T (eds), London: Hodder and Stoughton.

Marre Committee (1988) *Report on the Future of the Legal Profession*, London: HMSO Books.

MORI (Market and Opinion Research International) (1980) *The Teaching of Law-related Studies in Secondary Schools*, London: The Law Society.

National Consumer Council (1989) *Ordinary Justice*, London: HMSO Books.

National Curriculum Council (1990) *Curriculum Guidance 8: Education for Citizenship*, York: NCC.

Porter, A (1991) Address to Citizenship conference held by Runnymede Trust and Institute of Education, Nov 1991.

Rawls, J (1972) *A Theory of Justice*, Oxford University Press.

Rodin, P (1992) 'A Cross-Curricular Approach to Personal and Social Education', *Pastoral Care in Education*, 10, 1, March.

Rowe, Don (1987) *Evaluation Report on the Law in Education Project*, London: The Citizenship Foundation.

Rowe, Don (1990) 'Crime in the Classroom', *Citizenship*, (the Journal of The Citizenship Foundation) 1, 1, pp 19–22.

Rowe, Don (1992) 'Law-related Education: an Overview' in *Cultural Diversity and the Schools*, Modgil, S, Modgil, C and Lynch, J (eds), vol 4, pp 69–86, London: Falmer Press.

Scarman, Lord (1981) *Report of an Enquiry into the Brixton Disorders*, London: HMSO.

Torney, J V (1971) 'Socialization of Attitudes Toward the Legal System', *Journal of Social Issues*, 27, 2, 137–154.

Vorhaus, G (1984) *Ignorance of the Law: A Research Report*, London: Hillingdon Legal Resources Centre.

Part Two: Citizenship and Voluntary Action

Chapter 4

Citizenship and Community Service Volunteers

Elizabeth Hoodless

Young people do not become good citizens by accident, any more than they become good nurses, or good engineers or good bus drivers or good computer scientists. Citizenship, like anything else, has to be learned.
[The Rt. Hon. Bernard Weatherill, MP]

INTRODUCTION

Since 1962 Community Service Volunteers (CSV) has involved over three million people as 'active citizens'. CSV empowers them to care for others, to monitor and expose pollution, to form action groups, and to enrich schools. CSV believes everyone, young and old, has something to give; no volunteer is ever rejected. Some care for frail, elderly and disabled people, others tackle inner-city dereliction, others help tenants to organize to improve their estates, and many care for homeless people.

CSV's aim is to enable every individual to become a citizen, not just by voting every five years but through making a direct difference to our communities. The significance of their role is reflected by the absence of involved citizens in nations such as Ceausescu's Romania or Albania. Those appalling orphanages and psychiatric hospitals would not have been tolerated had ordinary people been involved as volunteers. Direct involvement in all aspects of society is a critical element of citizenship, curbing excessive state action or neglect.

Gallup surveys show that over half the British population gives voluntary help each month somewhere: many more than those who vote, as Chris Patten (1990) pointed out in his pamphlet *Big Battalions and*

Little Platoons. Volunteering is a central bulwark of our society, a democratic right that is being increasingly exercised. CSV encourages that growth through six key initiatives.

CSV VOLUNTEER PROGRAMME

Each year over 2,500 young people (16–35) serve full-time, in hospitals, schools and women's refuges, or caring for individual disabled people, enabling them to live independently. They receive board, lodging and pocket-money and experience the fun, adventure and challenge of direct action to change someone's world. For many it is their first chance to take responsibility for another person. The experience often raises profound concerns about society as a whole and their personal responsibilities. In 1992, 30 years will have passed since the first CSVs started work: their lives testify to the impact of the experience. One is in Turkey leading the Overseas Development Administration task force for Kurdish Relief; another, also a doctor, is transforming the care of mentally handicapped people in Wessex; and a third is revolutionizing managers' attitudes to those they aim to lead. A survey by Public Attitude Surveys (1975) revealed that this experience caused over 90% of participants to form or clarify their own political views and increased their election participation rates; critically important in a period when turn-outs drop annually.

CSV EDUCATION

Since 1969 CSV has pioneered the involvement of pupils in service related to their studies: by 1987 independent and maintained schools nationwide had pioneered challenging programmes, led by Sevenoaks School and Northampton Education Authority. The arrival of the packed National Curriculum threatened to terminate the initiatives: indeed the Secretary of State announced the abolition of the much-valued GCSE in Citizenship. (Happily, it emerged that he did not have the power to do so.)

Nevertheless, in 1988 CSV launched the Speaker's Commission on Citizenship under the patronage of the Right Honourable Bernard Weatherill, MP. The report, *Encouraging Citizenship*, was widely welcomed and led to the *inclusion* of citizenship in the National Curriculum for 5–16-year-olds. Some have been surprised by the involvement of primary pupils, but the opportunities are waiting to be grasped. For example, at Pakeman School, Islington, pupils in Key Stages 1 and 2 plan, chair and organize their own school council and negotiate issues of concern with the head, such as lunch-time procedure and the quality of toilet paper. The critical question is *how* is citizenship to be learned? To quote the Speaker again: 'Tell me and I forget. Show me and I remember. Involve me and I understand.'

At a time when youth membership of political parties is collapsing and thousands of young people are declining to appear on the electoral register, for fear of poll tax demands, it is critical to ensure that all young people *understand* the costs and benefits of being a citizen. This is unlikely to be achieved within classrooms.

The overriding priority is to discover and implement active *involvement*, for this is the only effective way forward. Since there is no slot on the timetable labelled 'Citizenship', the challenge of introducing, monitoring and recording citizenship is immense. The National Curriculum Council (NCC) offers one page: five steps towards complex development through nine subject areas. Just as important is the whole life of the school: of course, as the NCC suggests, pupils can 'observe' a local election. But how much more effective to run their own at election time. And why limit it to election times? The National Union of Teachers (NUT) and CSV are cooperating with a north London borough to promote democracy in schools by involving pupils in reaching decisions about areas of concern: lunch-time arrangements, discipline procedures or playground litter. No doubt questions will arise about curricula, governors and power and authority inside and outside the school. The complexity of the challenge needs a 'John Harvey Jones': a report is due in 1994.

The major challenge of citizenship education is how to organize it across subject areas but without specified time allocation or cash resources. A team of teachers from Warwickshire and Waltham Forest is developing a handbook and training pack to help schools ensure that all their pupils and students are involved in every aspect before they leave. To be effective, the involvement must be active learning. For example, 11-year-olds at Denby High School, Clwyd, visit a housebound person *en route* to school each day and collect shopping or prescriptions. Over four years they have saved six lives through prompt action. In the process they have learned a great deal about their community and its oral history and gained awareness of economic issues and of family and public services.

UNCOMFORTABLE QUESTIONS

The questions that arise from this kind of learning may lead to some uncomfortable questions on which pupils must have the chance to reflect: for example, why do so many elderly people live in poverty? Why is the home-help service so limited? What is the boundary between state and individual responsibility?

Some time ago, pupils at Crown Woods Comprehensive in South

London were working at a local old people's home, where the residents were distressed by the removal of their false teeth. The students asked 'Why?' Their teacher encouraged them to talk to the matron. 'It's the rule,' she said. 'Who makes the rules?' they asked. 'The Director.' So the pupils invited him to school and he explained it was 'the committee'. The Social Services Chairman was intrigued by their request for an interview and shocked by what he heard. The teeth were returned. Thanks to their courageous teacher, that class learned many citizenship lessons. It might not be so easy if the geography group discovered that the river's pollution originated in the factory of the chairman of governors!

Another example of empowerment comes from the West Midlands, where a zebra crossing was awkwardly placed. Pupils therefore did not use it and an accident occurred. A distressed GCSE English student decided to take action: she identified the problem, wrote a report and made a speech to the Road Safety Committee, all course requirements. So effective was she that the crossing was actually moved, an achievement of which many MPs would be proud. In another instance, sixth-formers in Shropshire successfully campaigned to keep a railway station open.

Many, many opportunities arise for practical citizenship education, but teachers need to draw them out from pupils. It is also important to involve the community as a whole in the process; recognizing their role in citizenship education.

In 1989 the Council of Islington Sixth Form Centre was distressed by the theft of the seventh mountain bike: students wanted strong bicycle racks, like those provided outside public buildings. When they contacted the appropriate neighbourhood office, far from being invited to write a report or make a speech to the appropriate committee, they were assured that 'all would be well'. Nothing happened. Exams came, students left and citizenship education took a step backwards. Like thwarted school councils, cynicism may quickly set in. We must involve the whole community: councillors and MPs, planners, parks superin-tendents, playgroup leaders, police officers, solicitors and social workers are just a few of the people who are likely to be happy to talk to students and help them identify opportunities for action in which they can participate directly.

Undergraduates, too, can become active citizens; through 'Learning Together' thousands nationwide are tutoring pupils in inner-city schools. Pupils achieve more, tutors improve their communication skills, the community is enormously enriched. Overseas students have a particular contribution to make, especially in helping British young people understand the nature of citizenship in other countries. At Coventry Polytechnic, CSV pioneered curriculum-related action: undergraduate lawyers represent poor people at tribunals, student architects help tenants revitalize their estates and computer wizards help social services reroute meals on wheels. Both sides benefit: citizenship becomes active. Of course, many students volunteer already in a multiplicity of ways: CSV's distinctive approach is to relate the student's skill to the need, developing a mutually beneficial partnership: participation should benefit volunteers by improving their performance, as lawyers, architects or systems analysts. The challenge of citizenship education is immense, its importance beyond dispute. Without it the very survival of our democracy is at risk.

CORPORATE CITIZENSHIP AND EMPLOYEE VOLUNTEERING

Many companies contribute cash to the community. CSV encourages them to give much more: for example, IBM's City office has been linked with Stoke Newington school, exchanging computer training and work-experience placements for paintings and school play tickets. In Leeds, IBM personnel, at all levels from carpenter to site manager, have helped residents of Bell Isle to transform it from a 'sink' to a sought-after estate, sharing their skills of planning, fixing and negotiating. NatWest personnel in Islington give over 30 hours each week to children at Winton Primary School. Research demonstrates that employees' output does not fall as a result of volunteering; on the contrary, their commitment rises.

More and more employers are recognizing increased effectiveness in individuals, teams and companies when employees are involved in community enrichment. CSV's role is to link employers and employees with those needing help. The outcome, as we have seen with school governors, is a much more aware and better-informed electorate. Indeed, as in the USA, companies are beginning to raise directly with governments concerns about, for example, homelessness or education which employees have pointed out.

SENIOR VOLUNTEERS

By 2100, half the UK population will be of retirement age: already many senior volunteers are keen to share their time, experience and expertise. In Yorkshire and Somerset, older people help primary pupils to read. In Brixton, housebound ethnic minority seniors enjoy visits and outings with volunteers their own age. Brent seniors are following up poll tax demands to help people sort out their response. Changes in the National Health Service have opened up new challenges for senior volunteers; general practitioners are now charged with health promotion. Practices in Southampton and Glasgow are deploying senior volunteers to follow up failed appointments, help mothers get to clinics and check that patients are taking their medication on a daily basis. Such a level of support would be impossible without volunteers. Nationwide, over 1500 seniors are working through self-organized neighbourhood groups of 10–12. CSV provides leadership, training and stationery, while the seniors' average weekly commitment is four hours. Research in the Children's Hospital in Boston, Mass., indicates that involvement in active citizenship – volunteering – reduces blood pressure and cholesterol levels and prolongs active life (Kohn, 1988). CSV aims to involve over 2000 seniors by 1993: the main focus is on community care, environmental protection and education.

CONCLUSION

Some might ask: is CSV organizing Her Majesty's subjects to fill the holes left by government cutbacks?

CSV aims for much, much more: to enable every individual to become a citizen, through making a direct difference to our communities. When the former Home Secretary, Douglas Hurd, made speeches about 'active citizenship', he was calling for more people to become school governors, to support schools and to join Neighbourhood Watch to support the police. CSV goes much further: it challenges everyone to give some time, energy and commitment to enrich our society. CSV is working towards a compassionate society where every member contributes personally, not just paying taxes and voting every five years, not just supporting state services, but sharing their time, talents and expertise to enrich the lives of individuals and society as a whole. Their contribution may take many forms according to their age and availability; it may also include 'whistle-blowing' to draw attention to delinquent polluters or human injustices.

At his presidential inauguration, J F Kennedy, addressing his fellow Americans, said: 'Ask not what your country will do for you, but what you can do for your country.' CSV aims to help citizens find the answer, and act on it.

REFERENCES

Kohn, Alfie (1988) 'Beyond Selfishness', *Psychology Today*.
Patten, C (1990) *Big Battalions and Little Platoons*, Tonbridge: Charities Aid Foundation.
Public Attitude Surveys Research Ltd (1975) 57457, London.
Report of the Speaker's Commission on Citizenship (1990) *Encouraging Citizenship*, London: HMSO.

Chapter 5

Citizenship, Voluntary Organizations and the State

Roy Manley

THE GOOD CITIZEN

In 1988 when Margaret Thatcher threw 'Citizenship' into the political arena, Peter Kellner wrote in the *Independent* (17 October) that active citizens in the Prime Minister's judgement were:

> In the main people who are contributing to the success of free-market economies. Some do it directly, as entrepreneurs; others do it indirectly, by picking up the pieces that the free-market system drops – helping charities, clearing litter, helping inner-city reconstruction.

While not disputing that these were worthwhile activities, he doubted that they should determine 'citizenship'. He argued:

> 'Active citizen' is a description that should include . . . people who want to remain members of unions at GCHQ or probe Peter Wright's allegations. . . . Citizenship is a concept that celebrates diversity and dissent. It is a precious, exhilarating, anti-establishment word, which powerful politicians the world over have tried to steal. Only in dictatorships and enfeebled democracies do they ever succeed.

This type of good citizenship is one that deserves serious examination. Good citizens cannot be only those who fit into systems, who express their altruism by caring for the less fortunate, who volunteer to be special constables or join the Territorial Army or the St John Ambulance Brigade or who become hospital friends, prison visitors or magistrates. Good citizens are also those who want to change things through:

> Actions that . . . affect the distribution of resources, status, opportunities and life chances among social groups and categories within the country and thus help to shape the general character and equity of its social relations. (David Donnison.)

While it is not appropriate here to discuss the nature of a democracy and the United Kingdom's claims to being one, it is important to stress the concept's two dimensions. The vertical dimension of democracy is that which through elections produces parliaments, governments, local councils and local authorities. Whatever the nature of these elections, they are inherently imperfect in two respects. First, they reflect the political mood of a particular time, sometimes of a period as short as a few days. Secondly, political parties are voted into office on a general programme, a packaage of attitudes to issues. People might well disagree with some of the policies of the party for which they vote. It might be argued that in elections in the United Kingdom there is a third inherent imperfection. This is the likelihood of a government or council being elected to office with a minority of the votes cast.

It is these shortcomings in the vertical dimension of the democratic system that makes the lateral dimension vital to a healthy, responsible and responsive society. This dimension is sometimes part of a formal system. The Economic and Social Committee of the European Communities is an example. With constitutional power only slightly less than that of the Parliament, it is a permanent consultative body representative of employers, trade unions and others, including consumers. The House of Lords, a nominated, unelected chamber of parliament, has a similar consultative role in Britain.

The lateral dimension of democracy in the United Kingdom, however, is almost entirely provided by elements outside the machinery of government, by employers' federations, by trade unions, by religious bodies, by the media, by voluntary organizations. It is their daily involvement with special issues, whether at a local or national level, whether informed by altruism or self-interest, and the influence they bring to bear on governments and local authorities that reduce the shortcomings of the electoral system.

Of these elements outside our formal government machinery, voluntary agencies are the most numerous and various. They cover the widest range of issues and attract a broad diversity of people to their programmes. They are regarded by many as a peculiarly British institution but it is one that has been successfully transplanted to most countries of the world and is now, for example, taking root again in eastern and central Europe and the Soviet Union. It is through voluntary bodies that many of the great reformers of the past have exercised their influence, and many British citizens today work for change.

A BRITISH TRADITION[1]

Charity, a much-denigrated virtue, runs through the history of voluntary organizations, and charities – a precise legal term – are the most significant bodies in that history. Woven into it too, although not so closely now, was the Christian church. The Bible gives us the story of the good Samaritan, but the Samaritans, a body counselling those in despair, is a lay body.

From the eighth century monasteries were founded for the relief of the poor. From the 12th century charities established educational institutions – Balliol College in Oxford, for example – and hospitals – the first, Saint Bartholomew's, in London. In 1423 Richard Whittington, the Lord Mayor of London (and the Dick Whittington of pantomime), bequeathed a trust for the old and poor, which lasted for five centuries.

The early 16th century saw an increase in the numbers of those begging for a living. A survey in 1517 showed 1000 in London alone. In 1536 begging licences were introduced and able-bodied beggars were to be punished and returned to their parishes.

The preamble of The Elizabethan Statute of Charitable Uses of 1601 defined charitable uses or purposes and, although the statute is now repealed, this preamble still stands in the Law of Charity (see below).

In the 17th century a number of schools were founded as charities, including Alleyns in Dulwich and Merchant Taylors in Crosby. Almshouses were built, the Society of Friends (or Quakers as they were popularly known) was established and the Missionary Society for the Propagation of Christian Knowledge was started.

Thomas Coram, a successful mariner, set up the first children's charity in 1741, his Special Hospital for Foundlings, which, as The Thomas Coram Foundation in Bloomsbury, is now a successful pioneer in child and youth care. In 1750 the first charity performance to raise money for good causes took place. The great theatrical figure David Garrick, for example, produced Shakespeare's *Twelfth Night* in aid of the Middlesex Hospital. Towards the end of the century William Wilberforce began to lead the campaign that was to result in the abolition of the slave trade, and he founded The British and Foreign Anti-Slavery Society.

Voluntary bodies flourished in the 19th century as the problems of a new urban industrial society multiplied. Many were concerned with children's welfare. As pressure for a state educational system for the poor increased and the government began to subsidize charitable societies for the first time (in 1833), Lord Shaftesbury founded his Union of Ragged Schools. In 1851 a shoe-black brigade of 30 boys at the Great Exhibition at Crystal Palace cleaned 101,000 shoes and earned £500 for the Union, an exercise that was the forerunner of such fundraising events as the old Boy Scouts' 'Bob-a-Job' week and sponsored walks. In 1867 Dr Barnado started the charity that still bears his name, offering an 'ever-open door' to homeless children. The Young Men's Christian Association was set up in 1844 and its female equivalent in 1855; the Salvation Army, as 'The Christian Mission to Heathens' was launched by William Booth in 1865.

With urbanization too came housing associations, the Peabody Trust for example, and model settlements like Saltaire in Yorkshire. Rich businessmen like the Cadburys and Andrew Carnegie established trusts that are still active in promoting social welfare. A number of outstanding women reformers – Josephine Butler with her work for prostitutes, Elizabeth Fry with her concern for conditions in prisons, Octavia Hill, active in providing housing – brought increasing attention to Britain's social problems. Surveys by Charles Booth in London and Seebohm Rowntree in York showed how great these problems were. University settlements in London's working-class areas brought the young privileged into direct contact with the poor. Toynbee Hall in London's East End, for example, helped to fashion the thinking of such notable academics and politicians as William Beveridge, the architect of the post-Second World War welfare state, Richard Tawney, the Christian socialist Professor of Economic History at the London School of Economics, and Clement Attlee, Prime Minister in Labour's great reforming government of 1945–51.

With this burgeoning of voluntary charitable activity came increasing demands that it should be subject to greater public supervision. An 1861 survey showed that there were 640 charitable institutions in London alone. Between 1820 and 1866 no less than 40 specialized voluntary hospitals had been founded. Lord Brougham's work on charities and his conclusions that the country's charitable endowment should be recognized so that it could contribute more to the common good was followed in 1853 by the establishment of the Charity Commission as a watchdog over charitable activity. By the 1880s the Commission had approved some 4000 schemes for the reorganization of charities to make them more relevant to the demands of their times.

The decade before the First World War saw the establishment of the Royal Commission on the Poor Law (1905) and its recommendation that there should be a framework of state social services for the sick, the old, the unemployed, the mentally ill and children. The Liberal government acted on this and transferred the main responsibility for welfare from private charity to the state.

In the period between the wars local authorities assumed responsibility for slum clearance and housing and for help to disadvantaged groups. In the early thirties some voluntary bodies – the Workers' Educational Association, the Society of Friends and the National Council of Social Service (now the National Council for Voluntary Organizations), for example – helped in projects to relieve unemployment and its effects. Economic depression brought voluntary hospitals to the verge of bankruptcy. These hospitals generally charged for their services but often gave medical treatment free to those who could not afford it. The war years and the period of Labour government that followed it were times of great social reform. Lord Beveridge's Report *Social Insurance and Allied Services*, of December 1942, demanded that the state should be responsible for maintaining a minimum income and for upholding standards in education, health and housing. The Butler Education Act of 1944 introduced greater equality of educational opportunity and a tripartite secondary-school system. National Insurance began in 1946 and the National Health Service, with medical services free at the point of delivery, was launched in 1948. With the state at a national and local level now becoming a comprehensive welfare agency – in education, income maintenance, health, housing and the personal social services – voluntary organizations began to see their roles as pioneering new forms of social provision, bringing variety to the social system, offering alternative sets of values to those emphasized by the state, serving the interests of minority groups and giving people the opportunity to participate in matters that affected their quality of life.

The fifties and sixties saw the rapid growth of Third World charities, OXFAM having been founded in 1942. In the sixties self-help and community bodies were in the van of political pressure groups. The growth of unemployment in the late seventies and eighties, and the development of the Manpower Services Commission programmes, involved general and youth bodies in employment and training projects. State and local authority funding of voluntary bodies increased dramatically. It was in the late eighties, however, that government policies signalled what could be two major changes in the role of many voluntary organizations. First, while local and health authorities would retain the responsibility for seeing local services delivered, these services should wherever possible be provided by private or voluntary organizations on service agreements. What has become known as the 'contract culture' has hit the voluntary sector. Secondly, a growing emphasis on community rather than institutional care for those unable to look after themselves is putting an increasing burden on voluntary bodies concerned with poverty, young people, old people and the mentally ill or disabled.

That voluntary agencies will be able to meet these new demands is undoubted. Whether it is in their or the nation's interest to do so is another matter. What would good citizens do?

THE VOLUNTARY SECTOR [2]

Most major British voluntary organizations are registered charities and most registered charities are voluntary organizations. While the two terms are not synonymous (public – that is, private – schools are often charities but are not voluntary bodies), commentators on the nature and dimension of the voluntary sector often use charities as their yardstick.

At the end of 1991 there were some 210,000 registered charities. In 1985 registered charities had an income of £12.65 billion or 4.1% of gross national product. Of this about 25% came from public authorities. In 1987–88 central government grants totalled £293 million, local authorities £651 million, with grants from trusts of about £600 million and from business of £285 million.

Between 1971 and 1986 the number of members of the large environmental bodies increased dramatically, that of the Royal Society for the Protection of Birds from 98,000 to 506,000 and that of the National Trust from 278,000 to 1,417,000. The membership of Greenpeace (which is not a registered charity) is expected to reach 500,000 in 1992, having been a mere 5000 in 1980. It is estimated that over 23 million people participate in voluntary work and contribute the equivalent of 750,000 people's work on a 40-hour week. Paid staff are some 250,000. The voluntary sector, then, is a significant element in British society.

The National Council for Voluntary Organizations publishes an annual Directory of Voluntary Bodies with an English or United Kingdom remit. The Directory is alphabetical – from the Abbeyfield Society to the Zebra Project – but it also gives the organizations by area of interest. The range reflects society's concerns. There are no fewer than 59 subject categories, including Addictions, Animal Welfare, Arts, Blind, Children, Community Development, Consumer Affairs, Counselling, Deaf, Education and Training, Elderly, Emergency Relief and Refugee Services, Employment and Industry, Environment and Conservation, Equal Opportunities, Ethnic Minorities, Family Welfare, Health and Medicine, Housing and Residential Care, Human Rights, International Co-operation, Law and Justice, Mental Illness, Mentally Handicapped, Offenders, Physically Handicapped, Play, Rural, Self-Help, Social and Community Work, Transport, Women and Youth!

This is mirrored at a local level. The Oxfordshire Council for Voluntary Action's 1991 Directory has hundreds of entries; many bodies mentioned are the local entities of national bodies, but it also lists such purely local groups as Adventure Playgrounds, Allotment Associations, Animal Welfare Societies, Housing Associations and Trusts, Community Associations, a detached Youth Work Project, a Fieldpaths Society, Drop-in Centres, Hospital Leagues of Friends, Information and Advice Centres, a Nightshelter for Homeless People, a Local History Association and Recycling Groups.

While the voluntary sector's major areas of concern might change over the years, the increasing strength of environmental bodies being a recent example, its activities alter less rapidly: to give service, to pioneer new provision, to work with the disadvantaged, the vulnerable, ill and disabled people and minorities, to protect and develop a more caring and just society and a healthier environment, and to influence other sectors, notably governments and local authorities, in their policies and programmes. It is over the last of these that there is growing public debate.

INFLUENCE FOR GOOD

It was argued in the first section of this article that the voluntary sector is an essential element in the lateral dimension of democracy, which in turn is a vital part of the whole democratic process.

Three questions surround the role of voluntary organizations in influencing official policies and programmes. The first is: what political action is legitimate for a necessarily apolitical voluntary body? The second is: what is acceptable in the law of charity? The third concerns statutory funding.

What is not in general dispute is the right, perhaps duty, of voluntary agencies to promote views they believe favourable to their concerns. In 1835 De Tocqueville argued that voluntary associations were vital to save the democratic state from 'stultifying orthodoxy' and the individual from 'complete subordination to impersonal administrative machinery'. Lord Beveridge's 1942 report and his succeeding publications emphasized the importance of voluntary action as a means of social advance. The report of the Committee on the Law and Practice Relating to Charitable trusts, set up by Prime Minister Clement Attlee but reporting to Winston Churchill in 1952, and chaired by Lord Nathan, said *inter alia*:

> Some of the most valuable activities of voluntary societies consist, however, in the fact that they are able to stand aside from and criticize state action, or inaction, in the interests of the inarticulate man in the street. . . . This is one of the fundamental arguments for interposing this wealth of voluntary associations between the citizen and public authority, however enlightened and benevolent this latter might be.

More recently and specifically an inquiry into the activity of the National Association of Citizens' Advice Bureaux found that that organisation's use of case material to highlight major social and economic concerns was a necessary and legitimate activity.

What political action is legitimate for an apolitical voluntary organization? In the eighties, following widespread consultation, the National Council for Voluntary Organizations published a code for relationships between voluntary bodies and government. Two points in it merit mention. The first was the need for any political action by a voluntary organization to be in line with its constitutional objectives. An agency concerned with the relief of sickness should not attack the government's defence policy. Secondly, a voluntary organization should take pains not to be *party*-political, not to come out in support of a particular party that it might see as more sympathetic to its objectives. To these points of definition should be added the obligation on a voluntary organization to present its case with reasoned argument.

If a voluntary organization is a charity it enjoys two benefits denied to others. It has a measure of tax relief and it can seek money from those foundations whose constitutions forbid grants to non-charities. Charitable status is conferred and can be withdrawn by the Charity Commissioners.

As indicated earlier, the Elizabethan Statute of Charitable Uses of 1601 is now repealed, but its preamble is still used as defining charitable purposes. In part this runs:

> Relief of aged, impotent and poor people . . . the maintenance of sick and maimed soldiers and mariners, schools of learning, free schools and scholars in universities . . . the repair of bridges, ports, havens, causeways, churches and others.

In 1891 Lord MacNaughton reclassified these uses as

- the relief of poverty
- the advancement of education
- the advancement of religion
- trusts for other purposes beneficial to the community

The 1960 Charities Act laid down new responsibilities for the Charity Commission but did not provide a model legal definition of a charity. A committee on charity law set up by the National Council for Voluntary Organizations, chaired by Lord Goodman and reporting in 1976 also decided not to propose change in this area.

In Gerard's perceptive book *Charities in Britain* (1983), he points to some of the strengths and weaknesses of charity law. Rich and poor can benefit equally. Charity law favours beneficence and the established order. Of the charities surveyed for the publication two-thirds preferred social order to social change. Only one charity in 10 favoured radical social reform. Overseas aid, community work and social action voluntary bodies became most involved in politics.

A 1970s Charity Law Reform Committee advocated changes that would allow voluntary bodies to be charities without limitation on political activity.

In early 1992 a Bill on charity law reform was published. This followed a government White Paper from the Home Secretary (CMND 694), which itself was largely based on the Woodfield Report, *Efficiency Scrutiny of the Supervision of charities*. The White Paper concluded that there were 'few advantages in attempting a wholesale redefinition of charitable status'. The Charity Commission guidelines on political activity were useful and should be observed. Charities' governing instruments should not include a power to exert political pressure, unless ancillary to a charitable purpose, nor a power to bring pressure on a government to change or maintain a particular line of action. Propaganda should be avoided and balance maintained in education and research.

While difficulties and anomalies remain in charity law and its application, most people closely involved in voluntary bodies would probably prefer the present situation rather than run the risk of new definitions producing even greater constraints on political activity.

The third area of debate surrounds statutory funding of voluntary organizations. Should governments and statutory bodies give grants to agencies that criticize them? Most would argue that they should, but some would say that these grants should not be used for this critical role.

Some 20 years ago I was invited, as the head of a voluntary agency, to a ministerial reception. No one knew the reason for this last-minute invitation. Then, with drinks in our hands, the Minister announced that the Cabinet had that week agreed to give grants to our organizations so that we could mount public education programmes in constructive criticism of his department's work. Much more recently the writer was at another meeting with a Minister and was greeted with evident disbelief when he told him this. 'Surely,' the Minister said, 'no Government will fund criticism of its activities?'

A Home Office leaflet circulated in mid-1991 asks why central government helps the voluntary sector, and answers its own question thus:

> The aims and activities of voluntary organizations are frequently consistent with the Government's own objectives. This fact is recognized by many of the Government's funding regimes, which provide direct support to efficiently managed organizations.

There is a clear implication here that a voluntary body with aims and activities that might be seen as inconsistent with the Government's (that is, ruling party's) own objectives should not be officially supported in those aims and objectives. In an interview for a supplement to *NCVO News* in June 1991, Chris Patten, Chairman of the Conservative Party, appeared to contradict himself when he said:

> ... I have never believed that increasing the funding of voluntary organizations should inhibit them from being critical of the funder.

and then, a little later:

> Anything that looks as if it is the funding of political lobbying gets you onto very slippery terrain. I had this difficulty with aid agencies in

relation to development education. I felt it was awkward for them and for me if I put myself in a position in which I might have to justify apparent responsibility for their literature in the House of Commons.

Bryan Gould, interviewed for the same supplement as Shadow Environmental Secretary, said:

. . . It has been a great British tradition that in government you fund people whose job it is to make life difficult for you. I accept all that.

'A great British tradition' and one that, in the funding of voluntary organizations, could be as important as funding Her Majesty's Opposition.

CONCLUSION

It has been argued that good citizens are not necessarily only those who contribute to society as it is but also include people who want to change that society.

Democracy has two dimensions: the vertical (electoral) and the lateral. Lateral democracy, the day-to-day involvement of citizens in trying to influence programmes and policies, is an essential part of the democratic process, especially in countries that do not have proportional representation.

Voluntary bodies, most of them charities, have for centuries provided the means for social reformers to change society and continue to do so. The voluntary sector is now a considerable part of the British scene in terms of its income and expenditure, its range of interests, its membership and staffing and its volunteer contribution. While this is generally recognized there is less general acceptance of its role in influencing official policies and programmes. Here controversy surrounds such matters as voluntary–statutory relationships, charity law and government funding. This controversy is reflected in the different approaches of the major political parties.

Nevertheless voluntary bodies are – and will continue to be – vehicles of change, and being involved in them a way of expressing real citizenship.

NOTES

1. I am indebted to Anne Daltrop's book *Charities* for much of this section (see bibliography).
2. The statistics in this section are largely from National Council for Voluntary Organizations and Charities Aid Foundation sources.

REFERENCES

Beveridge, William (1948) *Voluntary Action as a Means of Social Advance*, London: Allen and Unwin.

CMND 694 (1989) *Charities: A Framework for the Future*, London: HMSO.

CMND 8710 (1952) *Report of the Committee on the Law and Practice Relating to Charitable Trusts*, London: HMSO.

Cook, C and Stephenson, J (1988) *The Longman Handbook of Modern British History 1714–1987*, 2nd ed, London: Longman.

Daltrop, A (1978) *Charities*, London: Batsford.

Gerard, D (1983) *Charities in Britain*, London: Bedford Square Press.

Gladstone, F (1982) *Charity Law and Social Justice*, London: Bedford Square Press.

Goodman, A (1976) *Charity Law and Voluntary Organizations*, London: Bedford Square Press.

Harris, M and Billis, D (1985) *Organizing Voluntary Agencies: A Guide Through the Literature*, London: Bedford Square Press.

Home Office (Voluntary Services Unit) (1978) *The Government and the Voluntary Sector*, London: HMSO.

Home Office (1991) *Government and Voluntary Organizations: Support and Partnership*, London: HMSO.

International Council on Social Welfare (1982) *Action for Social Progress: The Responsibility of Governmental and Voluntary Organizations (Proceedings of the 21st International Conference on Special Welfare 1982)* Vienna: ICSW.

Nathan, Lord (1990) *Effectiveness and the Voluntary Sector: Report of an NCVO Working Party*, London: NCVO.

Royle, E (1990) *Modern Britain: A Social History*, London: Arnold.

Sheridan, L A and Keeton, G (1983) *Modern Law of Charities*, 3rd edn, University College of Cardiff Press.

Whitaker, B (1984) *The Foundations: An Anatomy of Philanthropy and Society*, London: Eyre Methuen.

Wolfenden, J (1978) *The Future of Voluntary Organizations*, Beckenham: Croom Helm.

Part Three: Citizenship – International Perspectives

Chapter 6

Education for Citizenship in France

Hugh Starkey

INTRODUCTION

The whole of the French political and social system is founded on an explicit commitment to human rights. French schools have the duty and the fundamental task of producing citizens who understand and respect the constitution and the basic republican values of freedom, equality and solidarity (*'liberté, égalité, fraternité'*). The two-centuries-long tradition of educating citizens to be supportive of and knowledgeable about human rights continues to be a major concern of the French education system. The French curriculum details a citizenship and human rights education syllabus that is compulsory for all children from age six and continues to the end of schooling. There is a specific time allowance for this education, though it is also an essential part of subject studies, particularly in history, geography and French. This chapter sketches in some background, examines the formal syllabus and the official guidelines, and illustrates ways in which this education is supplemented by officially sanctioned local and national initiatives organized by voluntary associations and educational movements. It makes some comparisons with the English guidelines on education for citizenship and concludes that these should be strengthened.

HUMAN RIGHTS AND THE FRENCH CONSTITUTION

The French Revolution of 1789 marked a dramatic turning-point in the civil and political life of the nation. From being subjects of an absolute monarch claiming divine right to rule in an authoritarian and arbitrary way, French people became citizens firstly of a constitutional monarchy and then, in 1793, of a republic in which sovereignty lay with the people. This change is expressed in the Declaration of the Rights of Man and of the Citizen of August 1789, which affirms the essential equality of human beings and proclaims the fundamental freedoms of conscience, religion, opinion and expression. As with any declaration, including the Universal Declaration of Human Rights of 1948, the text is a statement of principles and intent and not a guarantee that the principles will be protected by law. However, as early as 1791 the text was adopted integrally as part of the new constitution, which thereby abolished 'irrevocably the institutions which denied freedom and equality of rights'.[1]

From the outset the Declaration, drafted in plain rather than philosophical language, was considered both as an educational text in itself and one that required to be widely known and explained: 'The representatives of the French People . . . have decided to set out in a solemn declaration the natural, inalienable and sacred rights of man, in order that such declaration, continually before all members of the social body, may be a perpetual reminder of their rights and duties.'[2]

As well as being a French text, the Declaration was assumed to have universal relevance. The first article states: 'Men are born and remain free and equal in rights.' The drafters were, of course, aware that Jefferson had already stated that all men are created equal, with certain inalienable rights, in the American Declaration of Independence of 1776. The sexism of the original formula was picked up at the time by Olympe de Gouges, who in 1791 wrote to the Queen with her feminist version of the Declaration, whose first article runs: 'Women are born free and remain equal to men in rights. . . .'[3]

In a sense, then, many French people, including public authorities, consider the notion of universal human rights to be a French gift to the world. Not only should all their young people be imbued with the spirit of human rights, but they should campaign with others anywhere in the world for the achievement of their rights. This feeling is all the stronger because the original ideals of the Revolution were crushed a decade later, to re-emerge briefly in 1848 and then more definitively only in 1871. There are many French people who well remember the suspension of the Republic in 1940 and the human-rights abuses perpetrated by the French Vichy government. There is consequently much awareness in France of the fragility of human rights and constitutions and the need both for legislation and education in order to guarantee them.

Surprisingly, the 1789 Declaration has not aged. It is to be found, intact, in the preamble to the current French Constitution, that of the Fifth Republic of 1958. 'The French people solemnly proclaims its attachment to Human Rights and to the principles of national sovereignty as defined in the Declaration of 1789 and confirmed and completed in the preamble to the Constitution of 1946.'

THE EDUCATION OF CITIZENS

Education in human rights and citizenship has a long and distinguished history in France. In the early days of the Revolution there were human rights festivals and pageants. At the time of the bicentenary, in 1989, publishers reproduced 18th-century board games designed to instruct the public about their rights. Primary school teachers of the early days of compulsory universal education (1881) were considered to be the shock troops of the Republic, with a mission to instil republican virtue into their charges. Something of this tradition survives, although the venerable 'civic instruction' has been replaced, since 1977, with 'civic education'. The current official instructions date from ministerial decrees of 1985, though the syllabus gradually worked through the system as a whole and detailed guidance for the secondary school was issued only in 1990.[4]

In both primary and secondary schools one hour per week is allocated to civic education. In secondary schools this is taught by teachers of history, geography or French. The syllabus is detailed and supported both by official nonstatutory guidance and by a variety of text-books and teachers' manuals, from which teachers are free to make their choice. The syllabus is direct and quite explicit in expecting students to come to a love of human rights and the Republic, while rejecting any notion of indoctrination or preaching. The helpful role of nongovernmental organizations and campaigning groups is recognized and joint projects encouraged. Syllabuses are published in paperback for parents and other interested persons.

CIVIC EDUCATION IN PRIMARY SCHOOLS

The official text first defines the aims of this part of education as helping children understand that 'they do not live in isolation, that they have a historical background, that they have rights but also duties. Having an essentially moral dimension, civic education should encourage honesty, courage, the rejection of racism in all its forms, love of the Republic.'

The instructions go on to indicate that the content should be presented in as lively a fashion as possible. Furthermore, teachers need to be personally committed to the attitudes it presupposes. They will look out for opportunities to use interaction in the classroom to illustrate rights and responsibilities. 'They will use daily incidents and behaviour as educational examples, will insist on cooperative behaviour, will help children to practise equal rights and to participate in the national and international campaigns of charities and humanitarian organizations.' A common commitment to human-rights values does not, of course, mean insisting on a particular line of thinking or belief. 'Civic education must never be indoctrination or preaching, rather it encourages responsibility and is always an education for freedom.'

The syllabus is set out as a series of headings, which are developed in text-books and the accompanying teachers' manuals. The topics are as follows:

Cours Préparatoire (CP) (= Y2, Key Stage 1)

Learning the basic rules for life in a community involves the development of a set of habits that are essential for civic life:

- rules of hygiene, safety and dress
- making an effort and gaining a sense of work well done
- respect for school property and equipment
- self-respect and respect for others; an enjoyment of personal initiative and responsibility
- acceptance of other people's rights, of race and gender equality, of individual dignity
- a sense of cooperation and mutual help.

The symbols of the Republic: Marianne, the national flag, the national anthem, the national holiday.

Cours Elémentaire (CE) (= Y3 + Y4, Key Stages 1/2)

The rules of life in the school community will now include a clearer understanding of their justification. There is a general introduction to the institutions:

- key concepts presented in the school context: for example, person, property, contract
- our country: national unity and identity
- the national motto: *'liberté, égalité, fraternité'*
- the right to vote and universal suffrage
- France, its President, the ministers and elected national representatives
- the local authority, the mayor and local councillors
- the school.

Cours Moyen (CM) (= Y5 + Y6, Key Stage 2)

A study of the main institutions of French society and the principles underlying them. France in the world.

- the Declaration of 1789

- the Universal Declaration of 1948
- freedoms (association, meeting, expression) and rights (to work, to strike) achieved since 1789.

French institutions
- the Constitution
- the law (Who makes it? Who enforces it? Who sees it is carried out?)
- administrative arrangements: national administration and the levels of local authorities.

French society
- the example of a major public service (for example, the post office, the railways)
- the concept of social security and examples
- the study of a voluntary organization
- information and opinion polls
- road safety.

France in the world
- the army and national defence
- Europe
- international relations and institutions
- the recognition of other cultures and ways of life
- the nation and the human family.

The citizen and the Republic

A COMPARISON WITH ENGLISH GUIDELINES ON CITIZENSHIP IN PRIMARY SCHOOLS

The English syllabus[5] is organized around eight themes, and there are a number of areas of overlap. 'A pluralist society' clearly links with 'Recognition of other cultures and ways of life'. 'Public services', for which the English examples are a library and a swimming pool, is close to 'a major public service'. But the French exemplar typifies the major difference between the syllabuses. The suggested study is of the post office or the railways, two national – indeed nationalized – industries. Whereas the French stress all that unites the nation, from symbols and mottoes to President and parliament, not forgetting democracy and human rights, the English syllabus chooses the local. English children are to study the neighbourhood and their own families. They look at local links with Europe and languages spoken in the local community. They are not expected to learn about the Queen nor about Her Majesty's Government, nor Her Majesty's armed forces. There is no mention of the flag, nor of the national anthem. In a country whose popular press, reflecting and reinforcing popular attitudes, thrives on the Royal Family, chauvinism and xenophobia, it is surprising that no formal attempt is made to explain and perhaps to justify the monarchy. French primary-school children are expected at least to be familiar with political and institutional aspects of national life. English children are shielded from such matters.

CIVIC EDUCATION IN THE COMPREHENSIVE LOWER SECONDARY SCHOOL (*COLLÈGE*)

For young people aged 11 to 15, the French education system provides a single type of school with a common curriculum, the *collège*. At this stage the history, geography and French syllabuses are all designed to promote an understanding of the contemporary world and civic education provides complementary but still compulsory studies, focusing even more on human rights. The following review of the syllabus is taken from the official nonstatutory guidance published by the Ministry.

General objectives for the *collège*

Civic education is an important part of the educational process at this stage, but many of the overall aims of the *collège* have a direct bearing on civic education. The Ministry states, for instance, that the curriculum should enable students to acquire the essential culture necessary to lead a successful life as worker and as citizen (p. 11).

The guidelines acknowledge the significance of the fact of approaching adulthood. 'At this period the child becomes an adolescent and should be helped to take those steps that will enable it to be a social being capable of participating in the life of the school and in life in society.'

The comprehensive and multicultural composition of schools is recognized, and teachers have to accept the responsibility for ensuring that this is taken into consideration. 'The fundamental knowledge that students acquire is made available through a compulsory national curriculum, which should be studied within the given allocation of time. Teachers are free to choose their own textbooks and adopt their own teaching methods. Classes are fully mixed and care must be taken to adapt teaching methods to the diversity within the class.'

Not surprisingly, given the French Cartesian tradition, there is a stress on helping students to develop logical thought. They should be able to refer to principles, observe rules, and order their thoughts. 'Habits of analysis and judgement enable students to perceive their place in a complex and evolving world and understand the changes that characterize our society and thereby be enabled to participate in it.'

Real education for freedom is considered to be based on knowledge of self and of a changing society. Such knowledge enables students to play their role in society and helps them to make informed choices about their future, both in terms of educational options and their place in society.

The basics continue to be of crucial importance at this post-primary phase, but for the French these are not only reading, writing and oral skills but also the understanding of images. The ability to use rules of grammar and spelling is, of course, essential. However, the ability to read images is equally important. 'Schools of the Republic, whose function is to train people capable of thinking for themselves – that is, citizens – must also these days train critical viewers of television.'

Civic education is an important opportunity area for progress in oral skills. By definition these can only be developed in concert with others, and the discussion and presentation of views practised in civic education provide an ideal context.

Specific aims of civic education

Although the overall mission of the *collège* is to help create informed and active citizens, the place of civic education within this framework is specifically justified:

> Civic education is an essential part of education in a Republic that guarantees fundamental freedoms. This education aims to enable students to develop a sense of the common good, respect for the law and affection for the Republic. Thus students need to be informed, that is knowledgeable about the rights and duties exercised by all citizens when they come of age.
>
> Civic education implies an understanding of the rules of demo-cratic life and its fundamental principles, a knowledge of democratic institutions and their historical background, and thinking about the conditions and means of respecting human beings and their rights in today's world: tolerance and solidarity, rejection of racism, a desire to live together in democracy. This education enables students to follow their own desire for freedom and justice and to face responsibly the problems and challenges of our time.

In a sense, civic education is seen as essential to the preservation of democracy and the Republic. However it is also more than that. In line with the universality of human-rights values, French civic education is also creating citizens of the world.

> As part of a scheme for the four years of *collège*, the aim is to help young people become aware and responsible citizens in respect of the challenges of our time, namely democracy, security and peace, human rights, development, the environment and cultural heritage.

The aims expect both knowledge and the ability to understand fundamental values and live them out.

The 'challenges of our time' are not uniquely French, but challenges for the world community as a whole.

THE SYLLABUS FOR THE *SIXIÈME* (Y7)

In this first year of secondary education there is an emphasis on the school community and the education service. The syllabus thus builds on students' own experience. The aim is to give students the feeling of belonging to a school community and a country ruled by law, and to enable them to understand the workings of a great public service – education. School rules are not, of course, the same as social or political rules, but there are useful analogies.

For the purposes of this education, citizenship is defined as being about relationships with the state and with other members of the national community who participate in democratic life. Civic education is intended to develop a sense of responsibility and a liking for collective action.

The school

This is allocated about eight weeks of study time out of 30.

- the right to education
- the school and state
- the organization of education
- the *collège* as a community and as a democratic organization (administration, rules, committees, delegates)
- respect for self and for others; respect for public and private property

The nonstatutory guidance comments that at this age we may expect self-respect and respect for others, founded on the notion of contract and respect for the law and democratically established rules, and respect for safety warnings, for public and private property and for nature. We can also expect students to take into account respect for the environment, to be prepared to listen to others, to communicate and to cooperate, and to acquire a sense of individual and collective responsibility. Clearly success in this undertaking will make life considerably easier for teachers and for schools.

There is some indication of the pedagogical approach that should be taken: 'The study of school life starts with a survey of places and people in it; their different roles lead on to the structure and organization of the school community. School rules are an example of a contract.'

There is at this stage a considerable emphasis on acquiring concepts and the language to discuss and identify them. For each element of the syllabus there is a basic vocabulary. 'By the secondary school, teaching needs to lead to the acquisition of key concepts and their associated vocabulary - for example, legality, law, citizenship, responsibility, security.'

Local democracy: the *commune*

The *commune* is the basic level of local government. There are some 36,000 of them in France. This study is expected to take about 22 hours, which is three-quarters of the yearly allocation of time. However, the guidance notes that 'because citizenship education is experienced as much as learned formally, there must be flexibility of timetabling to allow visits, surveys and joint projects with other subjects.'

As well as visits, the study of school and council documents is recommended, and also use of local media - radio, newspapers, television. Students should help to contribute materials. The town hall and local press should be contacted for free materials. The school library should be asked to make up dossiers and perhaps arrange an exhibition.

There is an emphasis on active learning. Project work involving cooperation and discussion is recommended. Local or school groups may also be involved - for example, development groups, UNESCO clubs, human-rights organizations and environmental and conservation groups. School cooperatives and links with school-based youth clubs are particularly helpful in expanding and building on what is done in class.

THE SYLLABUS FOR THE *CINQUIÈME* (Y8)

Local democracy: the *département* and the region

Diversity and solidarity of people

- different backgrounds, beliefs, opinions, ways of life; tolerance; rejection of racisms
  The rejection of racisms (in the plural, with different forms of racism to be spelt out) is to be studied by reference to the Universal Declaration of Human Rights (1948) and the French law against racism of July 1972. Examples should be taken from the media. There will be a special study of apartheid.
- unequal development: locally, nationally, globally
  Whereas regional inequalities are in the geography syllabus, the approach in civic education will be thematic - for example, food, health, education. The study of North-South links will stress

independence and the opportunities for citizens in the North to get involved in development issues.

THE SYLLABUS FOR THE *QUATRIÈME* (Y9)

The struggle for freedoms

- habeas corpus (1679)
- Declaration of 1789
- Universal Declaration of Human Rights
- European Convention
- Convention on the Elimination of all forms of Discrimination against Women
- the rights and duties of the citizen

Although students studied some of these basic texts at the end of the primary school, they are presented again in the context of the progress of human rights. An historical approach, it is felt, helps prevent this from being too abstract. The English and American contributions in the 17th and 18th centuries are acknowledged but, not surprisingly, the role of René Cassin in the drafting of the Universal Declaration is stressed. The reciprocal nature of rights and duties is emphasized: 'no individual freedom without collective restrictions, no free exercise of rights without commitment to the community as a whole'.

Freedoms in France today

- fundamental freedoms: conscience, expression, association, unions, press
- property
- the family: marriage, divorce, rights of children
- women's rights
- economic and social rights: work, health, social security
- rights and duties of foreign residents
- public opinion and information
- computers and freedoms
- recourse against arbitrary decisions; the ombudsman

At this stage the syllabus starts to cover some particularly controversial issues. The official guidance comments:

The family will be presented not just as an institution whose members are linked biologically or legally but also as a social group demonstrating solidarity and responsibility as well as reciprocal rights and duties. The teacher will illustrate related social, economic, cultural and demographic aspects and will stress that the freedom that characterizes relationships in today's families should not exclude the responsibilities members of a family group should feel towards each other.

The place of so-called immigrants in French society is one of the most controversial and explosive political issues in contemporary France, and this possibly accounts for the inclusion of the otherwise somewhat surprising heading 'The Rights and Duties of Foreign Residents'. The guidance explains that this

> will be an opportunity to consider the movement of people and the cultural, social and economic importance of migration and to recall that the legal mechanisms that govern the presence of foreigners in our country do not rule out the notion of hospitality.

This is certainly one area that will test the effectiveness of previous attempts to instil 'the rejection of all forms of racism'.

Europe

- the EC, its institutions and workings
- the creation of the community of Europe

This part is directly complementary to the history and geography syllabuses. The contribution of civic education will be to stress

> the institutional, social and cultural aspects, as well as the values shared by all Europeans and which underpin their institutions and their national life: freedom, democracy, human rights, solidarity with the Third World, peaceful resolution of conflicts.

This year's course of civic education is considered perhaps the most important of the whole programme, as it is directly concerned with human rights and fundamental freedoms. The official guidance states that human rights have three essential dimensions: the political, the moral and the legal. These are developed through objectives concerned with knowledge, understanding, attitudes and skills as follows:

> *knowledge:* of basic human-rights texts and of the way these are enacted in society and in daily life;
> *understanding:* of key concepts such as freedoms, equality, sovereignty, the law; of the philosophical background (natural law, individual thought, the search for universals); of written laws, which enable concepts such as freedom to become particular rights;
> *attitudes and skills:* the ability to analyse situations, to realize the ethical implications of an action and the possible means of redress; attitudes of tolerance, respect, responsibility and solidarity in school life, in personal relations and in society at large.

The guidance acknowledges that there are problems related to human-rights education at this stage, particularly:

- the technical and legal language of the formal documents
- the controversial nature of the cases studied
- students' difficulty in perceiving that their current freedoms are the result of a long historical evolution and their possible unwillingness to recognize and accept the restrictions of life in society

The guidance concludes that teaching methods must combine texts, principles, law and real-life examples in a permanent dialectic. In addition this year is an opportunity for students to debate, to make presentations and to listen to each other. Case studies and role-plays will be particularly useful.

THE SYLLABUS FOR THE *TROISIÈME* (Y10)

France, a republican state

- nation, state, republic
- constitution of the Fifth Republic: its institutions and their working
- law, freedoms and justice
- political and social forces
- the state budget; taxes; redistribution to those in need
- the role of the state and local authorities in economic life
- national independence as a condition for democracy and the spirit of defence, guarantee of peace

The political institutions of the two superpowers

International life

- independence and cooperation
- the French-speaking world
- international organizations
- the challenges of today: human-rights abuses, terrorism, confrontations
- one world: the diversity of cultures, international solidarity

Conclusion

- democratic values

At this level students are expected to be able to consider abstract notions and general principles. There is no specific official guidance provided, but there is a useful general section on human-rights education in the *collège*.

HUMAN-RIGHTS EDUCATION

Although this is an essential part of civic education it is also the responsibility of all subjects and particularly history and geography, where it is clearly built into the syllabuses. The official guidance maps human-rights education onto the history and geography syllabuses and onto the general aims of secondary education. It illustrates how human-rights education is part of cross-curricular themes, which in the French context are: safety, information, the environment and cultural heritage, development, health, consumer issues. It indicates human-rights issues within each of these topics and also shows how a specifically human-rights topic, the Universal Declaration of Human Rights, can be included within the cross-curricular themes.

French educationalists have played a leading role in the Council of Europe's programme of human-rights education, and the full text of the Recommendation of the Committee of Ministers of the Council of Europe on 'Teaching and learning about human rights in schools'[6] is reproduced in the official guidance.

French schools are able to bid for money for special projects known as *Projets d'action éducative (PAE)*. The official guidance points out that human-rights issues are commonly adopted for such projects, which are often undertaken with community groups such as UNESCO clubs, Amnesty International, the League of Human Rights and MRAP, an anti-racist organization.

A COMPARISON WITH THE BRITISH GUIDELINES ON CITIZENSHIP IN SECONDARY SCHOOLS

At Key Stage 3 there are again certain aspects in common: the study of the family, discussion of human rights issues, examination of local authority planning controls. However, the British guidelines lack the intensive study of human-rights documents and texts and the specifically anti-racist position taken by the French official guidance. At Key Stage 4 students study Britain's links with the world and observe a local election. They also debate and study equal opportunities issues and legislation. Like the French they look at the development of social services and the welfare state. Essentially, however, a political dimension and controversial issues are avoided as far as possible in the English guidelines, and this must raise questions about the effectiveness of the British syllabus in preparing informed citizens supportive of democracy.

One point of comparison is perhaps particularly revealing of the differences of approach. Both guidelines recommend working with voluntary groups, but whereas the French list contains human-rights campaigning organizations, the English list specifies youth organizations (Guides, Scouts, Outward Bound, Operation Raleigh) and first aid (Red Cross, St John Ambulance). Interestingly the French syllabus does not mention the police at all, whereas for the NCC 'the contribution of the Police Service is of the greatest importance, especially the involvement of the school community liaison officers in lessons and extracurricular activities.'

THE ROLE OF EDUCATIONAL MOVEMENTS IN CIVIC EDUCATION

The fact of such substantial official support for education for citizenship and for human rights does not mean that such education is done well. There are many in-service courses for teachers[7] and other opportunities for teachers to learn about effective approaches to what is undoubtedly for many a daunting task. Increasingly, such discussions are in the context of education for the enlarged European community.[8]

One movement that has been particularly active in supporting teachers in active learning approaches to human-rights education and education for citizenship in a European context is the Office Central pour la Coopération à l'Ecole (OCCE).[9] This movement, founded in 1928, is linked to the French, and therefore to the international, cooperative movement. Its two founder-figures were Barthélémy Profit and Célestin Freinet and their contributions represent two key dimensions in the movement's activities. From Profit comes the idea of the school or class cooperative. This is defined by the OCCE as: 'societies of pupils run by themselves with the support of teachers in order to carry out collective activities'.

Whereas in the early days of the movement this might have involved fundraising to provide basic school equipment for all, it now usually involves fundraising for a specific class or school project such as a school journey or camp, an exchange involving another country, a drama festival or making a film. The funds are administered by the cooperative, with pupils, including primary-school children, taking responsibility for accounts as well as for major decisions about the chosen project. Fundraising often takes the form of selling buns during school break or making and selling calendars at Christmas. One role of the OCCE locally is to act as external auditor for the accounts.

Freinet's contribution is the tradition of active learning and project work. This is an encouragement to classes and schools to be ambitious in what they undertake with their students. It is not uncommon for nursery-age classes to arrange international exchanges or visits or for schools to have their own radio station or regular newspaper. These activities are considered to help create informed and confident citizens, prepared to work collaboratively and democratically.

In practice, a primary school that is an active cooperative school will have class councils and a school council. A class council is a formal meeting with chair, secretary, agenda and minutes. It may meet for half an hour as often as twice a week, in class time, to discuss matters of common interest and to plan and evaluate special projects. Whereas the teacher may chair some early meetings, the idea is to hand all responsibility to the pupils themselves. Sometimes suggestions for the agenda are written in a book or on slips submitted in advance to the chair. There may also be a class suggestions box. Often the year will begin with the drawing up of a class charter, which specifies pupils' rights and responsibilities with regard to each other, to their work and to their teacher. It will be voted on and displayed prominently as a reminder.

Each class council will elect representatives to the school council. This deals with issues concerning the school community as a whole, such as special festivals or performances, playground equipment or moves to open-plan teaching spaces. The delegates report back to the class council. School councils or even class councils may invite local dignitaries such as the mayor to their meetings to help advance specific proposals needing community support or funding.

The OCCE is a national federation. Each *département* has a branch, often working from offices provided by the local education authority and with a teacher seconded to promote the activities of the movement. These are defined as:

> promoting in all schools and universities the idea of cooperation, which is active learning in moral, civic and intellectual education, in order to stimulate the spirit of mutual help and support, to stimulate initiatives for working together, to give a feeling and a liking for responsibility, and to enable the learning of freedom, democracy and human solidarity.

The movement organizes an annual national teachers' conference and publishes a magazine for teachers and another for school children.[10] It promotes national competitions and projects, such as the human-rights and French Revolution poster competition at the time of the bicentenary in 1989. The winning entries were displayed at main railway stations by the SNCF. In 1990 the OCCE set up a European cooperative schools network and in 1991 and 1992 it is concentrating on making the terms of the United Nations Convention on Children's Rights known to children and to the public. The OCCE claims 45,000 cooperatives, three million members and 100 full-time workers.

There is another Freinet movement in France, the *Institut Coopératif de l'Ecole Moderne* (ICEM). This publishes attractive resource books for all ages and newsletters and materials for teachers.[11]

SUPPORT FOR CIVIC EDUCATION FROM LOCAL AUTHORITIES

In addition to the support of education authorities, through premises and staffing, many town or city councils take their responsibilities to civic education for young people very seriously. There are now some 350 young people's councils in France, where this movement started at Schiltigheim, near Strasbourg. As an example, in Grenoble primary-age schoolchildren (9–11-year-olds) were invited to submit projects for improving the city environment for young people. A selection was made and the authors of the 59 best-presented and worked-out projects were invited to form the 'council'. This council's agenda was to consider five of the projects (selected by a committee) and vote on one to be implemented. The meeting was attended by the city's mayor, but chaired by the young participant, with the help of the City Secretary. Each project was presented by its initiator. The children finally voted for a careers information point. The children's council continued to meet to monitor progress and eventually propose further projects.

Other cities take different initiatives involving schools. Nîmes celebrated International Human Rights Day (10 December) with a major exhibition involving local human-rights groups and a schools poster and poetry competition on the theme of human rights. Orléans celebrated the Convention on the Rights of the Child with an artistic competition for schools. The winners painted a mural in one of the public rooms in the city hall.

CONCLUSION

Although the great majority of French people consider school education to be above all about getting access to a good job or career, there is still a substantial group of 15–20% for whom civic education and the transmission of values are the main priorities of schooling.[12] It is almost certainly fair to assume that the great majority of French people would put civic education among their priorities for schools. In contrast, it is unlikely that most British people would have a clear idea of what education for citizenship entails. They would not, for the most part, link citizenship and human rights.

The British tradition has, on the whole, been rather more mistrustful of political and civic education than of sex education, and it is probably a more controversial issue. There has been no lack of activity and voluntary effort by teachers in promoting education for democracy and human rights, though this has occurred within movements such as development education, peace education and global education. These initiatives, however, have received little support or recognition from official sources over the past decade and the political, human rights and democratic dimensions are played down within subject studies in the National Curriculum and even within the guidance on education for citizenship. On the other hand, official support for economic and industrial awareness within the curriculum has been considerable, in spite of the fact that these dimensions too are potentially politically controversial. It is as if British young people are to be protected from confronting and understanding democratic debate during their schooling.

French schools are encouraged to take citizenship education seriously from an early age and local politicians are prepared to play their part in supporting education for democracy and human rights. With its 36,000 local authorities, France has a high proportion of elected representatives and its people participate strongly in elections. French children are not shielded from explicitly political dimensions, though they have guarantees of freedom of conscience and their teachers may not promote specific political views in a school context. Importantly, French children study major national and international charters, declarations and conventions that provide the framework for continued democratic freedom in Europe and its eventual extension throughout the world.

The study of human-rights conventions can be made interesting for young people and should be a compulsory part of their school experience. All such international charters assume that governments will make efforts to make the contents known and the school system is ideally placed to undertake this task with young children. The Committee of Ministers of the Council of Europe acknowledge that 'human rights inevitably involve the domain of politics'. The Ministers go on to say: 'Teaching about human rights should, therefore, always have international agreements and covenants as a point of reference.' The English National Curriculum Council guidance on citizenship consequently seems surprisingly weak in its conclusion that 'Areas of study might include ... the major conventions on human rights.' Effective citizenship education for all requires changing that 'might' to 'will'.

NOTES

1. Preamble to the Constitution of 1791.
2. Preamble to the Declaration of 1789.

3. The full text can be found in Jaune, L (1989) *Les Declarations des Droits de l'Homme*, Paris: Flammarion.

4. The French national curriculum is published in two volumes as:

    Ministère de l'Education Nationale (1985) *Ecole Elémentaire Programmes et instructions*, Paris: CNDP.

    Ministère de l'Education Nationale (1985) *Collèges Programmes et instructions* Paris, CNDP.

    Guidance on civic education in lower secondary schools is provided in:

    Ministère de l'Education Nationale de la Jeunesse et des Sports (1990) *Education Civique: Éducation aux Droits de l'Homme, Classes des Collèges 6e, 5e, 4e, 3e. Horaires/objectifs/programmes/instructions*, Paris: CNDP.

5. This refers to National Curriculum Council (1990) *Curriculum Guidance 8: Education for Citizenship*, York: NCC.

6. Recommendation R(85)7 of May 1985.

7. For an account of one such, see Best, F 'Human-rights Education and Teacher Training' in Starkey, H (ed.) (1991) *The Challenge of Human Rights Education*, London: Cassell.

8. Examples are Scola, organized biennially in Rennes (1989, 1991 etc.) and the summer school in Geneva under the auspices of CIFEDHOP.

9. 101bis rue du Ranelagh, 75016 Paris.

10. *Animation Education* and *Delta Plane*.

11. Available from PEMF, BP 109, 06322 Cannes la Bocca Cedex.

12. Duhamel, O and Jaffré J (1991) *SOFRES L'Etat de l'Opinion 1991*, Paris, Seuil p 263.

Chapter 7

Education for the International Responsibilities of Citizenship

Patricia Rogers

The salvation of mankind lies only in making everything the concern of all.
[Aleksandr Solzhenitsyn]

We are beginning to discover that our problems are worldwide, and no people of the earth can work out its salvation by detaching itself from others. Either we shall be saved together or drawn together into destruction.
[Rabindranath Tagore]

Schools all over the world should pay more attention to international problems so that young people will see more clearly the dangers they are facing, their own responsibilities and the opportunities of cooperation – globally and regionally as well as within their own neighbourhoods.
The Brandt Report

CITIZENSHIP

A citizen is a full member of a community. In Roman times, people were either citizens or slaves. The citizens shared the responsibilities of creating and running their society; the function of the slaves was to serve the citizens. Many countries perceive the responsibilities of citizenship as so important that civics – the social science dealing with the rights and duties of citizenship – has a place on their timetables throughout their schooling.

The acknowledgement that all people should have full citizenship rights was enshrined in the Universal Declaration of Human Rights, adopted by the General Assembly of the United Nations in 1948. Article 1 declared that 'All human beings are born free and equal in dignity and rights. They are endowed with reason and conscience and should act towards one another in a spirit of brotherhood.' Article 3 declares that

'Everyone has the right to life, liberty and the security of person.' (United Nations, 1985.)

The Declaration has 30 articles, covering the rights of citizens and their responsibilities in safeguarding those rights for themselves and each other. These rights and responsibilities of citizenship can be summarized in three categories: social, political and civil (Speaker's Commission on Citizenship, 1990). Socially, all citizens should have enough health care, education and economic security to take full part in their society. Politically, citizens share in the exercise of power – for example, as members of bodies exercising such power, or as electors of those members. Civil aspects include freedom of thought, belief and speech, the right to make legally enforceable contracts and the right to justice in disputes.

Each of these elements of citizenship is supported by institutions. Social requirements are underpinned by the health services, education systems, social services and a range of voluntary and semi-voluntary organizations; political concerns are exercised, for example, through parliament and local government; civil rights are protected through the courts.

Each element of citizenship involves rights and responsibilities – rights for ourselves and responsibilities towards each other. To be effective citizens, we need not only to be aware of our own rights and the structures that exist to support them but also to be active in ensuring that our fellow-citizens enjoy their own rights. We need to be aware of how these rights can be undermined and of how to strengthen them.

Citizenship involves membership of a society. The concept makes sense for members of any group whose actions and decisions affect each other. The term is most often used about membership of a state. However, the concept is equally valid for membership of other societies. There are those that cut across states such as one's religious or professional group. There are small societies, such as one's family, school or town. Larger societies in which we share rights and responsibilities include the European Community, the North Atlantic Treaty Organization, the Commonwealth, and the largest of all, whose identity as an interdependent community is often stressed by calling it 'the global village'.

SOCIAL RIGHTS

Each citizen of the world has social rights that include basic health care, shelter, clothing, food, clean water, a reasonably safe environment and education. However, many do not have these fundamental necessities of life. More than one billion people (about a fifth of the world's population) live on less than a dollar a day (Clwyd, 1991). More than 35,000 children die each day (UNICEF, 1992).

If we share responsibility for this fate of our fellow world citizens, what are the structures and means available to us for tackling the scandal of global poverty?

The structures include the United Nations and its agencies, which work in health care, education, food programmes, international trade arrangements, international debt management, environment care, work with refugees, and many other international issues. We can express our concerns about its work through our national governments, through participation in associated voluntary organizations, and through direct lobbying.

The structures through which we can affect world poverty also include our governments, local and national. We can influence them by word of mouth, by letters, by supporting active groups, with our votes and through standing for election. If we feel that certain rules of our country – such as the tariffs that persuade poor countries to send us their raw materials for processing here, so that the main profits are made by us, not them – are not fair on our poorest fellow world citizens, we must make this point of view heard.

Another set of structures through which we can help are those of the voluntary organizations. There are those that work on international humanitarian, development and environment projects and also those that lobby national governments and international institutions on these concerns. We can support these organizations through our funds, our membership, or through supporting through their activities – such as by participation in letter-writing, workshops, and local community and media activities.

The structures available to us also include many aspects of our lifestyles, such as our involvement with commercial companies. These companies range from small community concerns to transnational corporations, some of whose budgets and power are greater than those of many states. They range from fair-trading and environmentally sensitive organizations to those whose overwhelming priority is profit, regardless of long-term environmental consequences or the welfare of workers and communities involved. We can become shareholders in these organizations and raise our concern that environmental consequences should be considered and that the poorest of our fellow world citizens should not be exploited. We can influence the companies through our power as consumers: every time we buy something, we are influencing a huge web of international relationships, which reaches the world's poorest.

The issues are not easy on a personal, institutional or national level. On the personal level, for example, should a responsible citizen buy tulips from Kenya to support the trade of that country? Is it good to support the growing of tulips to help Kenya earn the foreign exchange needed to pay off its international debts? Or is tulip cultivation for rich foreign markets taking good land that used to grow food for the local people? Is it leading to hunger, to more expensive local food and to food cultivation now having to be scraped from less fertile land? Are the nomadic herds that used occasionally to graze the less fertile land now having to graze marginal land that they are turning into a desert? Even if these effects are real, is boycotting the tulips an effective way of helping? Similarly, should the responsible citizen support a company that actively promotes bottle-feeding of babies in communities where it is a frequent cause of malnutrition and death (contravening the guidelines of the World Health Organization) – even when that company produces the best chocolate products available?

On a local level, when choosing new seats for its parks, should a local authority buy ones made from tropical hardwoods? They are good value for money. They will weather well. They will give income to people living in tropical forests. But their manufacture might contribute to the destruction of the tropical forests and to the greenhouse effect, damaging the global environment.

On the national level, should tariff barriers be put up to protect certain industries here – at the expense of those of poor people in other countries? As with most legislation on domestic issues, in such decisions there will be winners and losers. The key difference is that all the people involved domestically have the political power of voters, so their rights are all likely to get reasonable consideration. In national decisions that affect our fellow global citizens in other countries, we need to ensure that domestic considerations do not have a monopoly; our responsibility for our fellow-citizens to have the basic social necessities of life must be considered.

We have most responsibility for our fellow world citizens where we are most interdependent and where we have most influence. Whether we like it or not, many of our personal decisions affect people in other parts of the world. This is more obviously true of their social situation – in health, environment, education and economic security – than in their civil and political rights.

POLITICAL AND CIVIL RIGHTS

However, many of our national decisions do affect the civil and political rights of people all over the world. Our legal and political systems still have links with some of our former colonies; we are still in the process of decolonization for others, such as Hong Kong. As our links evolve, we have a responsibility to consider the interests of all those involved.

Nations, unilaterally and multilaterally, have sometimes imposed sanctions on countries as a protest against their internal political structures. The international efforts against South Africa's apartheid-based constitution are an obvious example. There have also been shorter-term, internationally imposed sanctions to try to uphold civil and political rights of certain groups of world citizens. For example, these were tried against Rhodesia, following the white regime's unilateral declaration of independence in 1965.

Other intergovernmental methods of ensuring the civil and political rights of people in other countries range from the pressurizing and bargaining behind closed doors that is an intrinsic part of international diplomacy to the full-scale force that was eventually used against Iraq following its 1990 invasion of Kuwait. In between there are: peace-keeping measures (often under the auspices of the United Nations, and usually intended to be temporary while attempts are made to find a mutually satisfactory long-term solution, as in Cyprus and Kashmir); the organization of plebiscites and elections (again usually by the United Nations, to help to determine the wishes of the people involved, as in Namibia and Nicaragua); and multilateral, humanitarian endeavours (such as for the earthquake victims in Armenia).

For those whose civil and political rights are breached in their own countries, there are extra-national courts of justice, at European and at global level. We share responsibility through our national and European governments for the terms of reference and efficiency of these in righting people's wrongs.

The United Nations charter starts with the words 'We the peoples', and we all share responsibility for the ways in which it works and the effects it has on people all over the world. This responsibility can be exercised in many of the ways already mentioned: through direct, personal contacts and lobbying; through support of active voluntary groups; through supporting political parties that share our priorities; through our influence on the doorstep and at the ballot box at election time; through personal involvement in the institutions concerned.

DEVELOPING THE SKILLS OF CITIZENSHIP

Being an effective citizen needs appropriate attitudes, knowledge, understanding, skills and experience. Developing these is a lifelong evolutionary process – like education. Like education, too, a basic foundation is best established while a person is growing up. Citizens-to-be need:

'empowering – in terms of knowledge, skills, information, time and well-being – to become effective agents in the world. They need opportunities – in terms of decentralization of both political and economic power – in which they can be effective agents, that is, citizens. Finally, they need to be provided with the required motivation to take the practice of citizenship seriously, in terms of performing the duties which they owe to the [communities] . . . of which they are members.' (Oldfield, 1990.)

The Speaker's Commission on Citizenship (1990) listed the skills and experiences that schools should help develop as necessary for effective citizenship:

- the capacity to debate, argue and present a coherent point of view
- participating in elections
- taking responsibility by representing others, for example on a school council
- working collaboratively
- playing as a member of a team
- protesting, for example by writing to a newspaper, councillor or local store.

THE INTERNATIONAL DIMENSION

'In 1976 the UK was signatory to the Paris Recommendation, which pledged educational time for the pursuit of international understanding, peace and co-operation' (Human, 1987). In 1977, the Department of Education and Science published a consultative document, stressing the importance of a strong international dimension in the curriculum, because 'we live in a complex, interdependent world and many of our problems in Britain require international solutions' (DES, 1977).

Aspects of the preparation by schools of young people to be effective and responsible global citizens include development education, environmental education, human-rights education, peace education, multicultural education and education for international understanding. In describing these, Robin Richardson, formerly Director of the prestigious World Studies Project and now Director of the Runnymede Trust, updated the fable of the blind people who each tried to describe an elephant – one after feeling the tail, another the trunk, another a tusk, another a leg, another the back. In the revised version, they are trying to describe 'elephant education', and come up with all the variations above. As with the parts of the elephant, none of the parts of 'elephant education' is enough on its own. For any of them to be fully effective, they need to be linked with all the others.

For example, multicultural education should include global awareness. 'The main arguments for a global dimension to multicultural education . . . might be expressed (Lynch, 1987) as:

- respect for persons cannot stop at Dover

- others are building multicultural societies and we can learn from them
- the struggle against prejudice and discrimination cannot be a solely national one
- the interdependence of peoples necessitates a global multicultural education
- the identification of "moral" behaviour necessitates a supranational concern'.

The aims of 'elephant education', or education for world citizenship, are summarized in some recommendations arising from the International and Multicultural Education (IME) Programme in Scotland (Dunlop, 1987):

- Every pupil leaving school should have an understanding of the nature and workings of the world, a world which functions as a system of interconnected parts, each vital to the wellbeing of the whole.
- Schools should strive to develop skills essential for world citizenship. Pupils should emerge from our schools able to communicate, process information and ask pertinent questions. They should know how to continue to learn on their own and how, when older, to participate effectively in local, regional, national and international affairs. Pupils should be introduced to the process of change and its many manifestations and be able to speculate upon likely developments (social and scientific) influencing the lifestyle of citizens in the late 20th century.
- Programmes in IME should imbue all citizens ... with the knowledge and an understanding of the global interdependence of the world's peoples and communities, and the relevance of such relationships to their local and national situation.
- For all pupils ... IME should lead to a recognition and appreciation of ethnic, linguistic, religious and cultural differences, and should aim to assist in the eradication of racism and all other forms of prejudice and discrimination.

TEACHER TRAINING

Education for international understanding, cooperation and peace and education relating to human rights and fundamental freedoms are unlikely to develop spontaneously in schools. This is why it is very important for teacher-education institutions that train new teachers and undertake in-service education to become strongly involved in 'international education'. To this end, they must incorporate an 'international education' dimension in their courses. This involves giving knowledge (the content) . . . but . . . knowledge is not enough. Much more important are the attitudes and commitment developed in teachers: attitudes favourable to the values that underlie international understanding and commitment to taking action to support peace, human rights and fundamental freedoms. (Florez, 1984.)

Teachers cannot expect to be experts on all the current issues on which their students will want to be informed. Part of their training therefore needs to be in how to discover what resources are available and how to make best use of these resources. A wide selection of excellent teaching material is available, and many voluntary organizations offer a range of other support to schools. Recent research in Wales (Hopkins, 1990) found that the vast majority (more than 82%) of teachers in training felt a need to know much more about what the voluntary organizations could offer, and more than 77% wanted to make their teaching more international.

All this applies not only to initial teacher training but also to in-service training of teachers. Voluntary organizations offer a range of services, including materials (books, videos, posters, computer programs, periodicals and exhibitions), speakers, and even the organization of complete workshops on, for example, anti-sexist policy, problem solving, teaching about human rights, or politics and development.

Teachers can find more about what is available through the educational press, through their local teachers' centres and development education centres, through membership of the individual organizations or through membership of a networking organization, such as the Council for Education in World Citizenship (CEWC).

CONTROVERSIAL ISSUES

As was found in a recent survey, 'a particular need is for resources and training which will enable teachers to feel more confident and more motivated to tackle areas which are presently seen by some as too controversial' (Greig *et al.*, 1987). Teachers are often chary about joining organizations whose main purpose is to be a pressure group – even though most of these organizations are very responsible about not using their education programmes directly to campaign. Indeed, such organizations are usually aware that education is not about being given the answers, but about learning what the important questions and the issues involved in them are. The danger of campaigning or even indoctrinating the students must not mean that controversial issues are avoided. On the contrary, an important part of the teacher's responsibility is to help the students learn, first, how to understand and then how to make up their own minds on such issues.

Education for Citizenship involves discussing controversial issues upon which there is no clear consensus. This makes it all the more important for pupils to have the opportunity to acquire knowledge, to develop a respect for evidence, to clarify their own values, and to understand that people hold different, equally legitimate points of view. It is essential that such issues are presented to pupils in a balanced way, which recognizes all the views. . . . Where political issues are brought to the attention of pupils, there is also a duty to ensure that they are offered a balanced presentation of opposing views. (Williams and Sterling, 1988.)

Not only should education enable students to make their own informed opinions on controversial issues, it should also help them to understand other people's. In the words of the Scottish IME Project, education should lead to:

- consciousness that one's own perspective on world issues and other people's is biased by one's own cultural background
- empathy (viewing other societies from their own perspectives and one's own society from the perspective of others)
- appreciation of others, sympathy for the plight of the unfortunate, regard for the achievements of the creative
- ability to communicate with others across cultures without prejudice to oneself, and, also to combat prejudice in others

STRUCTURES FOR DELIVERING GLOBAL EDUCATION

The development of international understanding, which should be one of the end-products of teaching about world problems, is not a purely cognitive process. Therefore education for this purpose should aim not only at the communication of knowledge but also at the formation of attitudes and patterns of behaviour which will endure in adult life. (Abraham, 1973.)

To develop such attitudes and patterns of behaviour, they must permeate the whole curriculum from the very start of schooling. Global education is not something that can be taught in occasional, isolated periods, while other lessons use different approaches, attitudes and behaviour; nor is it something that can be started later, when other habits and attitudes have been established. Much of the specific information future world citizens need to acquire will be learned in particular subjects – but the attitudes and many of the skills need to cross subject boundaries.

According to Beverly Anderson (1991) 'Human knowledge is a rope which we unwind into subjects for our convenience, because it is easier to absorb complex matters if we consider them separately. But we use that knowledge every day by twisting the rope together again'. There are different ways of untwisting the rope, but certain characteristics should be visible in all the strands. These include multicultural and international understanding. To be effective, not only do the appropriate attitudes and skills need to permeate the entire life of the school, they also need to be explicitly worked on in all subjects.

There is scope for focus on these dimensions in all the National Curriculum subjects. There is not room here to go through the various programmes of study and attainment targets showing all the opportunities for emphasizing global perspectives. Some practical suggestions in GCSE English, History, Geography, Art, Technology, Mathematics, Chemistry and Modern Languages, as well as in the Certificate of Pre-Vocational Education (CPVE) and the Technical and Vocational Education Initiative (TVEI), are given in *Citizens of the World* (Council for World Citizenship, 1986). An analysis of the National Curriculum – with a page for each subject and cross-circular theme, showing the opportunities for the introduction of an international perspective in England and Wales – is given in CEWC's *World Dimensions in the National Curriculum*. The pages are loose-leaf, so the document lends itself to whole-school planning or monitoring across the key stages, as well as supporting individual subject teachers.

CRITERIA FOR GLOBAL EDUCATION

The working party that produced *Citizens of the World* pointed out that

> Education deals with values, concepts, information, knowledge and skills, as applied to people and human relationships and to our cultural and physical worlds. Good teaching is concerned with such matters as accuracy, integrity, fairness and effectiveness in communicating, and therefore also with methods and materials. The factors which mark good education are all prerequisites for education for international understanding. (Council for World Citizenship, 1986.)

They went on to note the additional factors that apply specifically (though not exclusively) to education for international understanding. They divided the criteria into two sections: awareness and processes.

Criteria concerned with awareness: education should enable pupils to:
1. empathize and give respect, allow dignity, recognize solidarity across national, religious, cultural, ethnic, class, sex or age differences, etc.; 2. recognize areas of conflict and their origins; 3. be open and receptive to 'other' ideas as possibly valid, and be able to assess them knowledgeably in their own terms; 4. be determined to meet the

world with realistic expectation, hope and welcome rather than suspicion, fear and resentment.

Criteria concerned with processes: education should enable pupils to:
5. be confident and competent in working in political terms – dealing with competing interests, group identities and dynamics, and power structures – and see how such forces work in local and wider situations; 6. lay a foundation for conflict resolution by identifying and seeking to understand opposing positions; 7. evaluate claims concerning rights, freedoms and duties in the particular situation in which they are made, and identify possibilities of change.

The awareness that education should prepare students for their responsibilities as global citizens needs to permeate the whole life of the school or college: its relationships with its community and wider world; its structures, attitudes, internal relationships and procedures; its extracurricular activities; all its curricular work.

SOME PRACTICAL SUGGESTIONS

Information

To make the decisions of responsible citizenship, people need accurate and up-to-date knowledge, as well as the skill of knowing how to find appropriate information in the future. Students need practice in effectively using newspapers, broadcasts, libraries, and the information put out by pressure groups. Broadsheets put out by CEWC, and other regular publications, are a useful source of information on topical issues.

But the information is not enough. We have to bring it alive and make it relevant for the students. There are specific activities that are particularly valuable in strengthening this dimensation.

Roleplay, simulation and games

In roleplay the participators try to adopt the attitudes and behaviour of other characters. Roleplay thus provides a memorable way of understanding issues – particularly those over which there is conflict.

Simple roleplays that can easily be introduced into a normal lesson are part of many teaching materials in the humanities as well as being a popular part of English and drama lessons. For example, groups of students might take the roles of different actors involved in reaching a controversial decision. Each argues its case. This highlights the different priorities and perspectives that may be held – quite legitimately – by negotiators, and often shows that there is no 'right' answer; difficult choices and compromises may have to be made.

A computer can take this further by allowing the groups actually to make decisions and then to seek the consequences. For example, the Centre for World Education Development has produced a computer-based roleplay simulation called Sand Harvest. The participants take the roles of nomads, villagers and government officials in the Malian Sahel. Away from the computer they negotiate: for example, the government officials might persuade the villagers to grow cash crops to earn foreign exchange – perhaps by offering to immunize their children. Each has limited power – the government officials over their budgets, the villagers over their time and the nomads over where they go – and many pressures on them. At the end of each year's decisions, the computer shows them the results of their actions on their families, animals, money, food, environment.

A similar build-up of the effects resulting from a combination of change and the decisions of several different characters is vividly portrayed in games like Gaining Ground, Oxfam's board game about land and harvest in East Africa. These and many other games and simulations are available through the Centre for World Development Education.

Roleplay can be used to help students understand points of view with which they strongly disagree. For example, in model United Nations activities (Security Council meetings, Committees or even full Assemblies), students take all the roles, including those of countries whose views they might condemn – such as, for example, Iraq when it had just invaded Kuwait, or China after the Tiananmen Square massacre. Model UN events give opportunities to develop all the skills of citizenship cited by the Speaker's Commission on Citizenship (1990), quoted above. They take place in many countries of the world. Taking part in an overseas UN model General Assembly with students from many countries brings international issues vividly to life in an unforgettable way.

More stylized simulations can be most effective ways of raising awareness of a wide range of issues, such as how we communicate, who has power, how we relate to people different from ourselves, or the structure of international trade. An Experience-Centred Curriculum (UNESCO, 1975) describes a range of these. It includes the well-known Four Hands on Clay, illustrating some of the processes involved in cooperative decision-making between two people.

Another particularly popular simulation for raising awareness of the structures of world trade is Christian Aid's Trading Game (1986). In this game each group represents a country. Paper, 'money', scissors and geometric instruments are shared in a specified – and uneven – way; the groups trade in precisely specified shapes of paper at given prices, each trying to make as much money as possible. The groups with the technology (scissors and geometric instruments) tend to make large amounts of money at the expense of those with the raw materials.

An important part of all roleplay and simulation exercises is the 'debriefing', or discussion at the end. Once the students can control the anger or other strong emotions that often arise (such as the sense of unfairness instigated by the Trading Game), their sense of involvement can be channelled effectively to analyse and understand the issues being illustrated. Normally slow learners become just as involved, and can participate in such experiences and their follow-up on equal terms. This can help to overcome their common reluctance fully to participate. All participants have the concepts concerned brought memorably to life.

Conferences

Conferences involving more than one class start with the advantage of breaking the normal routine. If they can include another school (particularly one of a different type), the chances of widening perspectives are even greater. Conferences can be built round almost any subject. The involvement of the students in choosing the subject and designing and planning the conference will not only be excellent practice and exemplify some of the attitudes and processes described above, it will also increase their commitment to the success of the conference.

The balance between passive and active components is important. It is useful to have some expert input shared by all, such as a film, performance or speakers. A simulation or shared creative activity, such as painting a huge joint poster or creating a play, can involve everyone. Workshops need to have some purpose, such as to produce a proposal, petition, or analysis to be fed back to a plenary. If the whole conference can end with some resolutions for further activity, there will be an increased sense of involvement and achievement. All these help to bring the issues alive, and to develop the skills and attitudes necessary for effective citizenship.

Linking and exchanges

Linking involves 'ordinary people directly in the process of taking shared responsibility for the future of the world. As an educational medium, rooted in person to person contact and learning through experience, linking is loaded with potential.' (Batty, 1991.)

The vast majority of links and exchanges in which British schools take part are with Europe – more than three-quarters with France. But there is a growing realization that links further afield have an even greater educational and humanitarian potential.

Sometimes the initial justification is to strengthen modern-language learning. In the Secretary of State's National Curriculum Modern Foreign Languages proposals, it was stressed that:

> There are many ways in which cultural knowledge underpins language proficiency and is acquired progressively as the language is learned. Social relationships and moral values, religious beliefs and political attitudes, historical, artistic and literary traditions, these all find expression in the idioms and structures of a language.
>
> Knowledge about the culture of a people refines and deepens understanding of the distinctive patterns of meaning in the language they speak. The teacher has a key role in helping pupils to develop cultural awareness and understanding. It is, for example, important to guard against creating or reinforcing stereotypes. (Welsh Office and DES, 1990.)

What better way of avoiding stereotypes, and of getting to understand a culture, than to have a friendly and growing relationship with a community in that culture? Whether their language is English or a modern foreign language (a European one in its home base, or as spoken in another continent, such as Francophone Africa or Hispanic South America, or a non-European language), enrichment of the appreciation and use of language will be one benefit. But there are many others; they permeate the whole curricular and extracurricular life of the school or college.

> At some stage, links usually include some exchanges of students. Exchanges enable pupils to broaden their outlook, giving them new exposure to another . . . culture which is quite impossible to convey in the classroom alone, offering real-life situations to be dealt with and real problems to be solved. School exchanges can enhance any or all areas of the curriculum. (Schools Unit News, 1991.)

However, exchange is not an essential component of links, although one does want an immediacy which can be difficult when depending on the post. But exchanges can be expensive and time-consuming and face some physical constraints, particularly, for example, for the handicapped. One alternative is through electronic mail. Campus 2000 and other networks, or direct computer links, can be used for this.

Linking and exchanges are usually arranged between pairs of scholars or colleges, but these are not the only possibilities. The Associated Schools programme of UNESCO has more than 2000 schools in 94 countries, committed to programmes of international understanding. By joining this group, a school gains a worldwide network of friends with whom it can exchange information, material and visits. More than 40 schools and colleges in Britain are currently ASPRO members, gaining these benefits.

Another scheme links schools and colleges (or others) to development projects in the South. This scheme of cooperation action (or Co-Action) is organized worldwide by UNESCO. The Northern partner raises funds and chooses from a catalogue of projects the one(s) to be supported. By exchanging funds raised for United Nations Units of Money, or UNUMs – with no deductions for administration – they are all given to the Southern project. The educational material that comes back from the project can be the focus of a wide range of educational activity – even including visits to the project. Co-Action is administered in Britain by CEWC.

Service

In many countries, all young people have a compulsory period of community service. While this does not apply in Britain, many schools realize the benefits such service can bring both to the students and to those who are served, and so include their own (compulsory or voluntary) opportunities for service. These activities can often have an international dimension, such as work with local immigrant or refugee groups, or involvement in international work camps, or working with an overseas school. Sometimes these community services are organized through extracurricular activities, like Duke of Edinburgh Award Schemes, Scouts, or Guides.

Many other organizations offer opportunities for young people after they have left school. Details of most of them can be found in *Volunteer Work*, by Hilary Sewell. She stresses that:

> The ideas and attitudes of volunteering once expressed as 'helping those less fortunate than ourselves' or as 'giving benefits to people in need' are at best inappropriate and at worst patronizing. Projects are essentially mutually rewarding and beneficial; both volunteer and co-worker are expected to be enriched by the experience of working on a common task and to have contributed positively, even if fractionally, to the betterment of mankind. (Sewell, 1986.)

The borderline between volunteering and working is often blurred, particularly for young people going overseas. Many opportunities for work and service overseas, for periods ranging from three days to a year, in any of 90 countries, for people aged from 12 years, are found in *Working Holidays Abroad*, from the Central Bureau for Educational Visits and Exchanges.

Local links

At the other extreme, a surprising degree of global awareness can come from looking carefully at one's own community. Interdependence then becomes a personally valid concept. In *Education for Citizenship*, such activities are suggested. At Key Stage 2 'pupils investigate links with

Europe which occur locally, for example, foods, words, goods and services, news articles, TV programmes, sport, holidays and pen-friends' and 'pupils conduct a survey of the languages spoken by members of the class/school and their families'. By Key Stage 4 'using a variety of resources, pupils investigate links Britain has with communities elsewhere in the world. They present their findings in the form of a report, media presentation or other suitable form', and 'pupils use a database of a recent census for the local area and identify where significant numbers of people were born.' (NCC, 1990.)

Other ideas

There are many other innovative ways of strengthening the international dimension of the curriculum. These can be in the classroom, in assemblies, in special events or in extracurricular activities. They include involvement in exhibitions, competitions, current events (such as Central America Week or Human Rights Day) and research projects on education for international citizenship. There are multicultural and international theatre, music and arts programmes on offer to schools and colleges.

One can participate in an existing link. For example, a British community or college might have a link with an overseas community or college. Sometimes nearby schools or colleges can take part – perhaps by hosting overseas visitors for a day, a week or a month.

Such opportunities are advertized in the educational press and in the circulars of many non-government organizations. A wide selection is offered in CEWC's bimonthly Newsletter to its members.

Conclusions

The Society of Education Officers and the Local Government International Bureau said recently that

> All sectors and organizations are being urged to think 'internationally' in preparation for the Single European Market in 1992. It is important, however, that we avoid the dangers of an inward-looking Europe – and here we must look for every opportunity to widen perceptions of citizenship in a global context and to explore the various international implications of these and other changes in the European scene, particularly for developing countries in the 'Third World'. (SEO/LGIB, 1989.)

As I have tried to show, such opportunities exist in abundance at all levels of education and however it is organized. They occur in specific topics in every subject of the curriculum, however these are defined. This might be according to English and Welsh National Curriculum subjects or might include subjects like humanities or the Scottish

'Modern Studies'. Similarly, there are opportunities within all cross-curricular themes – whether, again, they are relevant to the English and Welsh National Curriculum or include Northern Ireland's 'Cultural Heritage' and 'Education for Mutual Understanding'.

However, there is a danger that something that is everyone's job becomes no one's job. Careful monitoring is important. One possibility is to list some of the important topics that need to be studied explicitly, and to have a curriculum audit to ensure that they are all covered.

In *Global Connections*, Peter Batty (1991) describes an exercise carried out in Hampshire to help plan a multicultural curriculum. In this example, the topics considered were:

> literature about different cultures; cultural diversity in Britain; antisemitism; negative images in the media; human rights; stereotyping; race-relations legislation; biased viewpoints; colonialism/imperialism/exploitation; the Third World/development studies; racist language; slavery; apartheid; prejudice; different forms of racism; the art of different cultures; travellers; trade, multinationals and interdependence; immigration/emigration; speakers, visitors from British ethnic minorities.

Schools then looked at where and how these topics were covered in years 7–11.

Such checking mechanisms are particularly important in the last years of formal education, when students have options. Once certain subjects are dropped, a school or college needs to consider the international themes that all its students should address, and how it can deliver them. Assemblies, special days, whole-school or whole-year activities, a compulsory general or 'civics' course or module (like those that almost all othe countries in the world include) and extracurricular activities all have a role to play here.

It is not just some of our students who are going to have international rights and responsibilities: all are. All need to be aware of these and have the necessary knowledge, attitudes, skills and understanding to take on the international 'opportunities, responsibilities and experiences of adult life' for which their formal education has a responsibility to prepare them (DES, 1988).

As was said during the preparations for the 1992 Earth Summit in Brazil:

> The challenge of successful planetary management and development is enormous, as it entails both the collaborative development of truly sustainable and culturally appropriate models and the development of a politically acceptable strategy for implementing the model in everyday life. Environmental and development education is critical in both these phases of planning and implementation. . . . What is also

crucial is an environmentally aware and literate, and thus more responsible, society supporting the political decisions. (United Nations, 1991.)

We have a crucial responsibility in preparing the citizens of tomorrow's world for these challenges and responsibilities. This preparation is an integral part of their education. As the Swann report said:

a good education must ... give every youngster the knowledge, understanding and skills to function effectively as an individual, as a citizen in a wider national society and in the world community of which he (or she) is also a member. (Swann Report, 1985.)

REFERENCES

Abraham, H J (1973) *World Problems in the Classroom*, Paris: UNESCO.

Anderson, B (1991) 'Beyond the Worst Bounds of Human Thought', *Times Educational Supplement*, 12 April.

Batty, P (1991) *Global Connections: A Review of British Secondary School North-South International Links*, London: British and Foreign School Society.

Clwyd, A (1991) 'Labour Gears Up on Air', *Spur*, World Development Movement, April.

Commission on Independent Development Issues (1980) *North-South: A Programme for Survival* (The Brandt Report), London: Pan Books.

Council for Education in World Citizenship (CEWC) (1992) *World Dimensions in the National Curriculum*, London: CEWC.

Council for World Citizenship (1986), *Citizens of the World*.

Department of Education and Science (1977) Consultative Document, London: HMSO.

Department of Education and Science (1988) *Education Reform Act*, London: HMSO.

Dunlop, J (1987) 'Multicultural Education and Development: Convergence or Divergence?' in Human, R (ed.) *Swann and the Global Dimension: Education for World Citizenship*, London: Youth Education Service.

Florez, A Pendoza (1984) 'Implications for Teacher Education: The Content', in *Teaching for International Understanding, Peace and Human Rights*, Paris, UNESCO.

Greig, S, Pike, G and Selby, D (1987) *Global Impact: A Survey of Environmental and Development Education in Schools and in Non-Global and Statutory Organizations*, Centre for Global Education.

Hopkins, A (1990) *Development Education and Teacher Education in Wales*, Cardiff: University of Wales.

Human, R (1987) 'Global Perspectives and the Swann Report', in *Swann and the Global Dimension: Education for World Citizenship*, London: Youth Education Service.

Lynch, J (1987) 'Building the Global Dimension of the Multicultural Curriculum', in Human, R (ed.) *Swann and the Global Dimension: Education for World Citizenship*, London: Youth Education Service.

National Curriculum Council (1990) *Curriculum Guidance 8: Education for Citizenship*, York: NCC.

Oldfield, A (1990) *Citizenship and Community: Civic Republicanism and the Modern World*, London: Routledge.

Schools Unit News (1991) *Organizing School Exchanges*, Central Bureau of Educational Visits and Exchanges, Summer 1991.

Sewell, H (1986) *Volunteer Work: A Comprehensive Guide to Medium- and Long-term Voluntary Service*, Central Bureau for Educational Visits.

Society of Education Officers and Local Government International Bureau (1989) *Promoting International Perspectives in Curriculum Policy*, London: SEO/LGIB.

Speaker's Commission on Citizenship (1990) *Encouraging Citizenship*, London: HMSO.

Swann Report (1985) *Education for All: Report of the Committee of Inquiry into the Education of Children from Ethnic Minority Groups in the UK*. London: HMSO.

UNESCO (1975) *An Experience-centred Curriculum: Exercises in Perception, Communication and Action. Educational Studies and Documents 17*. Paris: UNESCO.

UNICEF (1992) *State of the World's Children*, Paris: UNICEF.

United Nations (1985) *Universal Declaration of Human Rights*, New York: United Nations Information Department.

United Nations General Assembly (1991) *Need for Environmental and Development Education. Paper A/Conf. 151/PC.21 of the Preparatory Committee for the United Nations Conference on Environment and Development*, New York: United Nations.

Welsh Office and Department of Education and Science (1990) *Modern Foreign Languages for Ages 11 to 16: Proposals of the Secretary of State for Education and Science and the Secretary of State for Wales*, London: HMSO.

Williams, R and Sterling, S (1988) *International Education: A Report on a Survey of Selected Oganizations Prepared for the Standing Conference on Education for International Understanding*, London: Council for International Education.

ADDRESSES

Campus 2000, Priory House, St John's Lane, London EC1M 4BX.

Centre for World Development Education, 1 Catton Street, London WC1R 4AB.

Council for Education in World Citizenship (CEWC), Seymour Mews House, Seymour Mews, London W1H 9PE. Director: Patricia Rogers.

Chapter 8

The Work of the United Nations

Malcolm Harper

INTRODUCTION

The United Nations was developed as a concept during the Second World War. Its role was to be stronger than that which had been given to the League of Nations after the First World War and its Charter was to be profoundly different from that of the League in a number of ways; but none so important as the outlawing of warfare as a means of settling disputes.

Against the background of two utterly appalling global wars fought in various theatres within a 30-year period, it was vital that a new and determined effort should be made to establish an international structure that would seek to end violence in inter-state relations and replace it with diplomacy and genuine cooperation. It is important to bear in mind that the United Nations was not set up as a form of 'world government' but as a voluntary association of sovereign member states, which were willing to work together to strengthen and to expand the body of international law that would guide and, indeed, govern the way in which they related to each other.

As World War II approached its end, it was envisaged that the countries of the world would agree to arm themselves lightly, so that they could defend themselves against the threat of aggression but would not have the strength to be an aggressor in the first place. Only three members would have larger armed forces: the Soviet Union, the United Kingdom and the United States of America. Even France, so I am told, would have been allowed nothing more lethal than rifles in its army – although who was going to break this news to Charles de Gaulle has never been made clear!

The theory was that any member state of the United Nations that felt itself under threat from another state would refer its fears to the United Nations. The situation would be reviewed by the Security Council, composed of a limited number of members. There are currently 15 members, including five permanent members: China, France, Russia (formerly the Soviet Union), the United Kingdom and the United States of America. They would advise the two potential enemies as to how best they might end their quarrel. As a last resort, the Security Council was empowered to enforce the peace by imposing economic, diplomatic and other sanctions against any member that refused to comply with its wishes; and, ultimately, to use military force, under the control of the Council, in order to achieve this compliance, if other measures had failed or were felt not to be appropriate in a particular situation. The complex occupation of Kuwait and its subsequent claim to have annexed it as its 19th province, was one of the very few examples of the use of this machinery since the United Nations was founded in 1945. Much controversy still surrounds what happened, as I will seek to explain later.

The tragedy for the world is that this idea of war-avoidance never got off the ground. No sooner had the Pacific War ended in August 1945 than the victorious allies, led by the countries that became the permanent members of the UN Security Council and were going to spearhead this new approach to international relations, began to move apart from each other. The Soviet Union was fearful of the intentions of the 'capitalist' world, which deeply distrusted the Communist government of Joseph Stalin, with its history of brutality and coercion. There was Soviet manipulation of elections in the countries of Eastern Europe in the later 1940s in order to get the Communist governments installed there, as a bulwark against the West. This and the Communist victory in China under the leadership of Mao Tse-tung threw the world almost instantly into what became known as the Cold War. All through the 1950s and into the 1960s, the increasing hostility of East and West meant that neither side was really prepared to use the United Nations and its machinery for war-avoidance in the ways that had been envisaged in 1945. The result was that the UN was largely stymied in its efforts to implement the Charter that had been agreed by the 51 founding member states in San Francisco and signed by them on 26 June, 1945.

This is not to say that the United Nations achieved nothing in those years. Although unable to promote a fuller peace in the world, it was nevertheless called upon to play a role – which proved to be very controversial – in the war in Korea from 1950–53, which began after China had helped the North Koreans to invade South Korea. Because of a dispute between the Soviet Union and the Western permanent members of the Security Council over something quite unrelated, the Soviet Union had temporarily boycotted meetings of the Security Council. Until 1971, the United States vetoed the entry of Communist China into the United Nations (the Chinese seat being held during those years by the defeated government of Chiang Kai-shek, based in Taiwan). The United States was therefore able, as a result of the Soviet absence, to get a resolution adopted in the Security Council that set up, under US command, a UN military peace-enforcement presence in Korea. The Soviet Union has never missed a Council meeting since!

More important for the UN was the setting up of the first UN

Emergency Force in the Middle East in 1956, following the disastrous Anglo–French intervention in the Suez Canal Zone – and a simultaneous Israeli advance against Egypt – in the wake of President Nasser's unilateral nationalization of the Canal. UNEF I, as the force came to be called, was put into position in the Sinai area of Egypt in order to ensure that the Israeli–Egyptian war should not flare up again. It was to stay in the area until 1967, when the Egyptians ordered it to depart as they prepared for war against Israel later that year. One of the basic weaknesses of UN peacekeeping forces (as such initiatives are called) is that their presence is determined – not least owing to arguments of national sovereignty – by the willingness of the country on whose territory they will be located to allow them in and then to stay. They can, as happened in 1967, be summarily dismissed by that host government. Nowadays increasing numbers of people ask whether, once a peacekeeping force has been agreed and put in place, its withdrawal should be decided on only with the joint agreement of the host country *and* the Security Council. This would be difficult to achieve but certainly merits very serious consideration.

There have been occasions when other groups have formed peace-keeping forces, and this is something that the United Nations has invariably welcomed. Examples of such initiatives include the regional support given to the government of Mozambique in recent years, the West African force in Liberia and Commonwealth inputs to conflict resolution.

Other notable UN peacekeeping operations have been mounted:

- the Congo (now Zaire) after the province of Katanga tried to break away and form its own independent state;
- in Cyprus, where it remains to this day and where it has helped very successfully to prevent ongoing violence between the Greek- -Cypriot and Turkish–Cypriot communities (a situation made much more complex than it already was by the illegal Turkish invasion of Northern Cyprus in 1974);
- in South Lebanon, where it has in many ways not been successful in curbing violence but where, very important, it remains a symbol of hope for the local population in all its trials and tribulations: and elsewhere.

GOOD OFFICES

Another vitally important aspect of the work of the UN Secretary-General is that of 'good offices'. In many areas of tension or violence, the Secretary-General has been able to offer his quiet help. During the missile crisis of 1962, the United States and the Soviet Union appeared to be on the point of war. The cause was the impending arrival in Cuba (which had just begun to be ruled by a Marxist government under Fidel Castro) of Soviet nuclear missiles. The quiet diplomacy of U Thant, the UN Secretary-General, helped to avert a disaster, as both President Kennedy and Mr Khrushchev later acknowledged.

A further, more recent, example of this role was the patient negotiating of the Geneva Accords on Afghanistan. The Soviet Union wanted a compliant state on its southern border to counterbalance the turbulence inside neighbouring Iran after the fall of the Shah in early 1979. It made the decision – appalling from every legal, moral and practical point of view – to intervene militarily in Afghanistan. During the early 1980s a fearsome war continued against Mujeheddin guerrillas, who had massive foreign military support, largely from the United States. While the Cold War continued, and even became exacerbated during the early years (from 1980) of the Reagan administration in the United States, there was no way in which superpower rivalry would let the United Nations play an effective role in seeking to bring the conflict to an end.

However, with the arrival of Mr Gorbachev in high office in the Soviet Union in 1985, the whole scene began to change. The frustrated good-offices work of the Secretary-General began to take off in an altogether more positive direction. It soon became very clear that the Soviet Union was keen to end its Afghan adventure as quickly as possible. Painstakingly, the Secretary-General and his Special Representative for the Afghan problem, Mr Diego Cordovez (from Ecuador), moved forward to discussions with the parties most closely involved. These were the governments of Afghanistan, the Soviet Union and Pakistan (where some three million Afghan refugees have been living for upwards of 10 years), with the United States taking a keen interest in what was going on. Finally, in 1988, the Geneva Accords were signed. Designed to assist the process of making peace in Afghanistan, the first step was to be the withdrawal (under UN supervision) of all Soviet forces from the country by the middle of February 1989. This was duly achieved; but, tragically, the fighting continued. There is no space here to describe with anything like justice the enormous complexities of political and social structures within Afghanistan. Suffice it to say that a permanent solution to this horrible war must lie with the people of Afghanistan themselves; but the United Nations is still, through its Good Offices Mission in Afghanistan and Pakistan, trying to help the search for that solution.

The United Nations has, over the years, also set up Observer Missions in flashpoints around the world. The UN troops on the Golan Heights on the Israeli–Syrian border; the UN presence for many years in Kashmir; the UN Verification Mission in Angola, which checked that the 1988 Accords were carried out (not least through the withdrawal of Cuban and South African forces there); and the first-ever UN presence, in terms of conflict resolution, in Central America; are all examples of this vital and creative UN role.

In Namibia, Africa's last colony, the United Nations Transition Assistance Group (UNTAG) had an enormously important part to play in the achievement of independence from South Africa's *de facto* colonial presence in the country in 1989. All interstate relationships have their complexities, but few can have been more difficult than the South African–Namibian story.

South Africa inherited, through the United Kingdom, the operation of the League of Nations Mandate, which was designed to help South West Africa (as Namibia used to be called) come to ultimate independence. The United Nations took over the old League Mandates, while South Africa, from 1948, started to adopt the system of apartheid. There was increasing tension within the United Nations, where as early as 1946 India had raised the issue of racial discrimination in South Africa. Finally, in 1966, the UN terminated South Africa's Mandate to administer South West Africa. In the early 1960s, the South West Africa People's Organization (SWAPO) had moved into armed struggle against the colonial authorities and a desultory war ensued for the next 25 or more years.

The unlawful South African intervention in Angola's civil war started as Portugal prepared to leave Angola in 1975 at the time of Angola's independence from colonial rule. The war was between two main rival political groups, the government and the rebel forces of the National Union for the Total Independence of Angola (UNITA). It looked as if it was going to come to a sticky end for the South Africans at the southern Angolan town of Cuito Cuanivale, where a major military defeat was staring them and their UNITA allies in the face. Rather than suffer this humiliation, the South Africans accepted the good offices of the US Government, which led to UN Accords on Angola. Confirmed by UN Security Council resolutions, the Accords led to the withdrawal of foreign troops from Angola (as already mentioned) and to the independence of Namibia, in keeping with UN Security Council Resolution 435 of September 1978. One condition of allowing South Africa a graceful withdrawal from Angola was its agreement to the independence of Namibia.

The UN Transition Assistance Group (UNTAG) in Namibia was at the very centre of implementing the independence plan. It was a very difficult plan to bring to fruition and the pathway to success was full of pitfalls. Nevertheless, free and fair elections were held in late 1989, a new constitution was negotiated and agreed between the various political groups that had won parliamentary seats in the election, and in March 1990 Namibia finally became unshackled from the chains of the apartheid regime.

In small, seemingly unimportant places like Western Sahara in

North-West Africa (which Morocco claims as its own against the wishes, almost certainly, of the majority of the inhabitants) and Eritrea, which has always disputed its forced integration into neighbouring Ethiopia, the UN has been asked to structure and supervise referenda in which the people can determine their future political status. This role may appear relatively minor in the whole ambit of global issues facing the UN, but to the peoples concerned they are highly significant; and if the UN is to be true to its Charter it must treat all of us with complete impartiality and equality.

Nowadays there is ever more talk of using the UN in the search for a more stable and peaceful world. The member states have all agreed on a UN-centred plan to stop the fighting in Cambodia, to hold free and fair elections there, and to help the people of that tragic country to find a real and lasting peace and true stability. At long last the Security Council has agreed a $1,800 million budget for this massive operation, which will, if it succeeds, be the largest-ever UN operation. Not only will the UN be involved with peacekeeping and disarming the four factions that have been fighting each other since the Vietnamese threw Pol Pot and the Khmer Rouge out of Cambodia in 1979; they will provide experienced civil servants to administer five key ministries during the period of their structuring and supervising of free and fair elections (scheduled for the first half of 1993). There are many complexities facing the UN in this delicate and bold undertaking, but it is breaking new ground in the development of the UN as a peacemaker, in keeping with the intentions of the founder members back in 1945.

THE 1990–91 GULF CRISIS: A TURNING-POINT FOR THE UN

There is little doubt that the Gulf crisis, sparked off by Iraq's invasion, on 2 August 1990, of its neighbour Kuwait, laid at the feet of the United Nations as great a challenge to its authority as any in its entire history. This was the first time that one member state of the UN had annexed another.

Opinions are deeply divided over the question of what role the United Nations should have played in the crisis. Some people believe that what happened in the region was correct; others that the UN was 'highjacked' by the United States, aided and abetted by the United Kingdom, as it sought to manipulate the machinery of the United Nations to achieve its own objectives. The truth, as is so often the case, probably lies somewhere between these two extreme viewpoints.

As soon as the news reached UN Headquarters in New York that the invasion, which had been threatening for some while, had actually taken place, the UN Security Council met and adopted Resolution 660 which:

- condemned the invasion;
- demanded that Iraq should leave Kuwait immediately and unconditionally;
- urged the governments of Iraq and Kuwait to settle whatever dispute existed between them through diplomacy and discussion.

In the following weeks, as Iraq announced first that it had annexed Kuwait and then that its position was basically unchangeable, a blockade was set up, aimed at preventing Iraq from importing or exporting anything. Iraq is almost totally landlocked, with its only access to the sea at the port of Basra, at the very top of the Persian Gulf in the Shatt-al-Arab waterway. Most of Iraq's neighbours disliked President Saddam Hussein, so it was possible to structure a relatively watertight blockade, by land, sea and air.

At the same time a number of foreign troops, including British and American ones, were sent to help to defend Saudi Arabia, since there were fears that Saddam Hussein might attack others of his neighbours. This was fully in keeping with the rights of member states acknowledge in the UN Charter. The number of troops deployed was such that they could only undertake a deterrent defensive role, being too few in number and armaments to consider offensive action. This was to remain the case until early November, when President Bush, apparently unilaterally, suddenly announced that he was preparing to double the number of American military personnel in the region, along with the armour that inevitably accompanied them.

This, of course, meant that the forces in the Coalition of states that had agreed to help Kuwait, Saudi Arabia and other countries in the area could now seriously consider offensive action in order to force the Iraqis out of Kuwait by military means. It was especially from this time onwards that politicians in the UK, the USA and elsewhere started to speak much more frequently of sanctions alone being insufficient to dislodge the Iraqis. Efforts by various groups to discover the basis for this assessment met with little adequate response. Then, on 29 November, the Security Council (in a majority vote, with China – a permanent member – abstaining rather than using its veto) adopted Resolution 678, which gave Saddam Hussein until 15 January 1991 to remove all his troops and civilian personnel from Kuwait or run the risk of incurring the military wrath of the Coalition forces. The resolution spoke euphemistically of using 'all necessary means' to secure Iraqi compliance with its demands; but few people doubted that this referred to military action.

The rest of the story is well known. For many people, however, there was a deep-rooted concern that Resolution 678, by authorizing military action after 15 January *outside* the control of the UN Security Council and its Military Staff Committee, had set a most unfortunate precedent – or even, in some people's minds, had transgressed international law. What had been authorized was the delegation of fighting to the US-led Coalition forces in the region. The decision whether to engage in hostilities was thus left ultimately to the US President and his military commander, General Norman Schwarzkopf, rather than to the senior military advisers of the UN Military Staff Committee and the Security Council itself. And when a pause – which led to a ceasefire – was authorized, it was President Bush who announced it, rather than the President of the Security Council or the UN Secretary-General. This remains one of the most controversial aspects of the whole debate on whether the UN acted wisely in adopting Resolution 678, as finally worded, or whether this was a major piece of manipulation by the United States and its allies to secure the consent of the UN to wage their own war.

The whole question of the future control of military enforcement measures, if, which God forbid, they should ever be needed again, is a key issue that must be actively addressed at the United Nations. For many people, such action should only be authorized by the United Nations itself and should remain under a UN military commander (who would, of course, have to be provided by a member state since the UN has no standing army of its own). These are complex issues, which cannot be discussed in detail here but merit much serious consideration and debate.

Way back in August 1990, at the time of the Iraqi invasion of Kuwait, the UN Secretary-General had been on a visit to South America. For reasons that remain unclear, he did not return immediately to New York, where the Security Council was meeting. His role in the follow-up to the invasion thus remained largely ill-defined, and he was less able to use his good offices to seek a diplomatic settlement of the dispute than would, almost certainly, have been the case if he had been present from the start. His absence also revealed once again the fact that there is no Deputy Secretary-General who could represent him. This is another area that needs to be evaluated, to ensure that the Secretary-General is given a central role in any future situation requiring skills in conflict resolution.

HELPING THE VERY POOREST

The United Nations Charter, adopted in San Francisco on 26 June 1945, recognized – quite rightly – that global peace and security would not be achieved by an absence of war alone but also by the eradication of poverty and injustice. History has shown all too tragically that violence and conflict are often caused by injustice and inequality. Prerevolutionary France and Russia showed what finally happens when the small élite band of 'haves' in a country ignore the rights and needs of the poor majority.

From the start, therefore, the United Nations has sought to play a key part in intergovernmental cooperation towards the fairer sharing of the world's resources and of human know-how. Through its specialized agencies – such as the Food and Agriculture Organization (FAO), which is based in Rome, the World Health Organization (WHO), based in Geneva, and the UN Educational, Scientific and Cultural Organization (UNESCO), based in Paris – it has brought governments and, increasingly, nongovernmental bodies into closer harmony and fuller cooperation in the battle against poverty, hunger, avoidable disease, illiteracy and social and economic injustice.

Other bodies within the UN tackle other specific tasks. The International Civil Aviation Organization (ICAO), with its headquarters in Canada, secures international agreements on aircraft overflying rights and a whole host of safety and other civil-aviation regulations. The Universal Postal Union (UPU), which is older than the UN but is now part of its family, secures agreement on international postal cooperation. The Office of the UN High Commission for Refugees (UNHCR) in Geneva protects the 17 million refugees in today's world and plays a key role in the meeting of their short-term humanitarian needs, their settlement in their country of asylum and, whenever possible, their eventual return to their country of origin. At the present time, the High Commissioner is having many problems caused by the ever tougher policies of so many governments towards refugees and asylum-seekers. The list of such bodies within the UN is seemingly endless – simply because the UN has been mandated to look after *all* aspects of the human situation all over our one world.

UNICEF, the United Nations Children's Fund, was founded after the Second World War to help child victims of that fearsome conflict. It has since then developed a global programme of helping children wherever they are in need of care and protection. It works closely with the World Health Organization on mother-and-child health strategies, plays a leading part in child immunization programmes, does much work – mainly with women – on child-spacing strategies and teaching what makes a sound diet for mothers and children; becomes involved with the provision of clean water for poor communities; and works closely with UNESCO in the area of basic literacy for children and, where necessary, for their parents. Like the UN High Commission for Refugees and many others in the UN family, it depends very largely on voluntary contributions from governments and ordinary people rather than on what are called 'assessed' contributions (which are compulsory) from UN member states.

Most recently, UNICEF has played the key role in securing the adoption in the UN General Assembly – the debating chamber of all 180 UN member states – of the Convention on the Rights of the Child. This lays out the minimum standards of child care and protection that should apply to every country of the world. UNICEF is now much involved in encouraging and helping countries to attain at least those minimum standards.

In the last two decades the UN has accepted the unique responsibility of promoting the concept and practice of global environmental care and protection. The United Nations Environment Programme (UNEP), based in Nairobi, Kenya, has been charged with the task of promoting environmental sensitivity and awareness throughout the whole UN system and the planning activities of the governments of the member states. Additionally, UNEP has set up a number of specific programmes to monitor environmental trends in such areas as the increasing size of the world's deserts, weather patterns and the like.

More recently, the United Nations has received a very important report, *Our Common Future*, drafted by a group of experts chaired by Mrs Gro Harlem Brundtland, the former Environment Minister, and now Prime Minister, of Norway. This major report has described in uncompromising terms the negative effects that poverty and pollution are having in our single world. It argues very convincingly that:

- environmental care and protection must be seen as global, with governments, communities and individuals all having a vital role to play in their achievement;
- poverty is the world's greatest polluter, which must be effectively tackled and eradicated through a massive global attack on its causes and the promotion of what the Report calls 'sustainable development' – that is, methods of production that will help to meet the needs of people today in ways that future generations will be able to continue to enjoy;
- the industrialized countries of the North produce the greater part of those pollutants that are causing global warming and ozone depletion, so that these countries must play the major role in combating these ills, while helping the development of poorer countries, through the promotion there of pollution-free technologies and the transfer of adequate resources to enable this to happen.

A very important UN Conference on the Environment and Development (UNCED) took place in Brazil in June 1992. Called the 'Earth Summit', it brought together governments and non-governmental organizations and sought to set the agenda for the next 10 years or more in the vital spheres of international environmental care and protection alongside sound and sustainable development strategies. Its success will depend, not least, on the *political* willingness of the rich countries to pay for the global strategies that the United Nations *must* pursue if that agenda is to be achieved.

SECURING BASIC HUMAN RIGHTS FOR US ALL

There is much more that could be said about the work of the United Nations in almost every corner of our lives; but since space is limited, this last section will look briefly at the work of the United Nations in the sphere of human rights.

The basis of this work is the Universal Declaration of Human Rights, adopted in the UN General Assembly – without a single negative vote (although some countries abstained) – on 10 December 1948. Later, the important International Covenants – one dealing with civil and political rights and the other with economic, social and cultural rights – were promulgated. Along with a whole host of other Conventions (we have already mentioned the Convention on the Rights of the Child), the United Nations has brought into being a very considerable body of international human-rights law. The importance of this achievement cannot be overstated, since without it there would be no common basis whatsoever on which to make judgements on the standard of human rights being enjoyed in the UN's member states.

Tragically, the willingness of governments to comply with this body of international law does not tally with their willingness to promulgate it. Time and again, countries are found wanting in terms of human-rights standards.

One such area is torture. Vital (nongovernmental) bodies like Amnesty International closely monitor and report on the incidence of torture in the member states of the United Nations. It is a sickening thought that, as late as the 1980s, the United Nations found it necessary to secure the agreement of its members to a Convention Against Torture because the overall situation around the world was – and remains – grim in this area. It is not just physical torture, as gruesomely displayed over the years in school textbooks and the Chamber of Horrors at Madam Tussaud's, which is widely practised; it is also psychological torture that has become popular: sleep deprivation, psychological pressures, prolonged periods of solitary confinement, death threats and the like.

The UN Human Rights Commission tries to monitor human-rights track records. It is not openly encouraged by many member states in its efforts to do so; governments are inherently loth to point the finger at another government, either at the UN or elsewhere, in case the spotlight swings round to expose some very nasty skeletons in their own cupboard. This widespread selectivity in which human rights issues to pursue manifests itself all too often, and has resulted in only a tiny percentage (0.7%) of the total UN budget being allocated to this area of work. When other parts of the UN family, such as UNESCO, seek to become involved in teaching human rights in schools, not many governments show any enthusiasm for their doing so.

In this situation, the staff members of the United Nations in general, and of its Geneva-based Human Rights Centre in particular, have always paid special tribute to the work of human-rights activists and nongovernmental bodies all over the world. In too many countries, such individuals or groups are harassed by governments: look, for example, at President Vaclav Havel and the Charter 77 group in Czechoslovakia in the years prior to the revolution of 1989. The UN and these other people and bodies have forged a vital and effective partnership to ensure that unsavoury governments do not manage to sweep human-rights standards under the international carpet. It is an area of ongoing challenge to the United Nations, which fully merits our unstinting support.

CONCLUSION

At the close of 1991, the term of office of the UN Secretary-General, Sr Javier Perez de Cuellar, came to an end. He was an essentially quiet man, but a very persuasive and determined diplomat, and by the end of his 10th and final year in office he had made a major contribution to the betterment of our world. Right at the end he had the pleasure of greeting John McCarthy and Terry Waite as they were released by their captors, and of achieving a breakthrough in the horrible civil war that had afflicted El Salvador in his home region of Latin America for so long.

He has been replaced by Dr Boutros Boutros-Ghali, who has already seen the United Nations grow in size to 180 members as the republics of the former Soviet Union and Yugoslavia, along with a number of other states, have recently gained admission to the world body.

This overview of the main areas of the work of the United Nations has sought to give a general feel for the world organization, its main areas of concern and how it tries to put into practice on behalf of us all the principles of the UN Charter. It has stressed that the achievement of this lofty aim is through the mobilization of adequate *political will* among the member states: a political will that is most likely to be seen at work when public interest in and concern for the effectiveness of the United Nations has become unstoppable.

It is to help to mobilize that public concern that United Nations Associations (UNAs) exist in over 70 countries of the world. In the United Kingdom, the UNA acts as an all-party parliamentary lobby group, undertakes educational projects about the United Nations in both the formal and informal sectors and acts as a general reference point for the dissemination of information about the UN, in close cooperation with the official United Nations Information Centre in London.

The United Nations will flourish fully when every one of us is determined that it should do so – and is willing to say so, for as long as it takes for this to happen.

Part Four: Citizenship and Education

Chapter 9

Developing Citizenship Awareness in Oxfordshire Schools

Neville Jones and Eileen Baglin Jones

INTRODUCTION

The responses received to any enquiry in schools about citizenship studies are characterized by wariness. This undoubtedly reflects an unease about this subject in general. In Britain there is a tendency to view work on citizenship matters in terms of local interest and possibly local participation. We find pupils, particularly in primary schools, encouraged to find out facts about their local environment. Part of this may involve pupils searching out the roots of their town or village, and sometimes their families. How did their own community develop and how did the community acquire its special characteristics in terms of population, industry, trade and commerce, voluntary groups, and leisure facilities? Emphasis here is often placed on local history. There is often a link with the local police force – Who is your local policeman? – and with matters of road safety or warnings about strangers. It is rare to find, at the primary level, any reference to national institutions, such as royalty, parliament, the armed forces, and national financing through government agencies. These are matters more likely to be found in the syllabus on citizenship for secondary-age pupils, but again the emphasis is likely to be on the 'facts' about democracy, legal rights and public services, rather than on questioning why certain institutions exist as they do, their place in modern society, and their contradictions with respect to certain features in our own or other societies in the world. There is a tendency to avoid debates about multicultural societies, the rights of minorities, the role of the police in a changing society, and the work of activist groups like Amnesty International. It is still difficult in secondary schools to launch programmes of study that address matters outside Britain itself – for example, the work of the United Nations, the European Parliament, International Relief Organizations, the issues surrounding refugees, the exploitation of natural resources worldwide, and abuses of the environment.

The National Curriculum Council (1990), in its publication *Education for Citizenship*, proposes, in general terms, a list of what the Council members regard as essential components of a citizenship syllabus. These touch upon relationships that create a sense of community, the diversities that occur in pluralist societies, and how, as citizens, there is a requirement for both duty and responsibility as well as civil, political, social and human rights. The NCC suggests five more areas in which teachers might with advantage explore the subject-matter of their citizenship courses: the family; democracy; the law; work and leisure; and public services.

There are few teachers who would argue with the inclusion of these topics in any plan to promote citizenship studies in their own schools. But each topic has enormous scope for interpretation, even in a presentation of the so-called facts. The setting up of the Speaker's Commission on Citizenship provided, therefore, an opportune occasion for some detailed study of the work being carried out in our schools in 1989 in relation to citizenship education. A national survey was carried out under the direction of Professor Ken Fogelman at Leicester University and was included as an Appendix in the Commission's report (Speaker's Commission on Citizenship, 1990). Some 57% of the mainstream secondary schools in England and Wales responded to the enquiry. The enquiry highlighted the very 'local' nature of activities pursued by the pupils – with the elderly, the disabled and people in health-care institutions, for example. It was difficult to gauge from a questionnaire enquiry of this kind just how regularly 'citizenship' activities took place in the lives of the pupils – that is, whether there was an ongoing commitment or just occasional interventions, when the activity was made a focus of the school syllabus. Although a number of schools reported that they had written statements or curriculum documents covering their citizenship studies, the topics and subjects dealt with seemed rarely to extend to what might be called political, civil and social rights and duties, in any controversial sense.

This is a reminder that in researching this area of the curriculum it cannot be taken for granted that everyone has a common definition of what citizenship entails. This is likely to be a problem in future research and curriculum development, whether by questionnaire, document studies, or structured interviews. Additionally, the value placed by a school upon citizenship studies, and hence its value as perceived by the pupils, depended upon the precise manner and context in which the studies were carried out. For example, in the Commission's survey it was found that some schools taught citizenship as a separate subject within the curriculum, others as part of other well recognized subject areas, such as history, geography, English and social studies. The survey revealed that citizenship was a theme or subject in personal and social education for some 95% of schools, and not all citizenship work was within the scheduled timetable but took place during form time or in tutorial groups.

Perhaps the most important finding in the survey relates to the extent to which schools provide 'active' learning in citizenship skills, by virtue of the way that the school itself, as a management unit, goes about its business and encourages participation. This is mainly in areas where pupils can be observers, or can participate, in school councils, governors' meetings, disciplinary procedures and parent groups, or as members of committees set up with the school to cover a wide range of matters relevant to an individual school and its corporate life.

This chapter attempts, through a brief description of a number of initiatives in Oxfordshire, to illustrate some of the difficulties inherent in considering 'Citizenship' in a clear and precise way as part of every pupil's entitlement curriculum, and some of the interesting and worthwhile issues in doing so. It also raises important questions about how schools can best play their part in the sometimes difficult task of ensuring that all young people become the kind of citizens society wants, needs and expects, without being open to the charge of social engineering and manipulation.

In parallel to the 'real-life' opportunities of pupils to acquire both an 'awareness' of citizenship matters, referred to above, and to experience it by participation, a number of schools have developed their own in-house schemes and opportunities. It is, of course, the case that many young people have experienced voting long before their 18th birthday, where there is a school council. The occurrence of a general election is also an opportune occasion to engage schools in matters relating to elections and parliamentary matters. During the period of the 1992 general election the Hansard Society for Parliamentary Government promoted throughout all LEAs a junior election in which pupils in participating schools could vote for candidates along national party lines. The Citizenship Foundation has also taken a lead in 'simulated citizen' activities through its Nationl Youth Parliament Competition. Schools taking part are required to produce video material on the working of the model parliament, such as question-time and debates. Another example of an attempt to raise awareness and give insight through practical participation in a simulation exercise can be found in the Magistrates Association schools project, which is gaining momentum across the country.

INITIATIVES IN OXFORDSHIRE

Citizenship initiatives in Oxfordshire have varied from school projects, as with the Banbury partnership of primary and secondary schools, to the work of the Oxfordshire County Advisory Service in providing a curriculum support pack for schools, a modular course on 'Citizenship' developed in association with the Oxfordshire Examination Syndicate Credit Bank and the Southern Examining Group, and the Model United Nations General Assembly simulation exercise for fifth- and sixth-formers, described in more detail later in this chapter.

The Junior Citizen of Banbury Initiative is a scheme introduced as part of a package of initiatives to facilitate primary–secondary transfers. The Banbury scheme is a development of ideas and practices put into effect in schools in Milton Keynes in the early 1980s, which were translated to suit the local circumstances of the Banbury schools. All pupils are given a 'Young Citizenship wallet', containing material that will provide them with guidelines about how to explore and learn about their local environment along citizenship lines (Cheer, 1991). Already this initial project is expanding, with additional material providing an industrial focus.

The Oxfordshire Advisory Service has in preparation a cross-curriculum support pack called 'Planning for Learning'. This is a difficult document to write, because of the breadth of the area to be covered and because it is extraordinarily challenging to offer advice about *specific* dimensions, skills and themes, which are at the same time so closely woven into the whole curriculum that they can only with difficulty be unravelled and treated separately. When one adds to this the fact that there is no real consensus about what a pupil's entitlement to the whole curriculum means, the scale of the problem grows even larger. The document from the Advisory Service explores issues related to the provision of cross-curriculum aspects of the whole curriculum, offers commentary and digests (useful short cuts for busy teachers) and examines ways of planning and of sharing good practice.

Pointing out that the National Curriculum can only be viewed as a basic curriculum, and that in all schools the curriculum is enhanced by, for example, out-of-school activities and the incorporation of cross-curricular themes, the advisers urge schools to recognize that there is much good practice already present. The recognition and utilization of overlaps between subjects and cross-topics will help achieve more coherence and less overload. The document examines the needs of a mature person, suggesting that he or she:

- needs to care for themselves physically and mentally;
- needs to support families and friends in these respects;
- needs to contribute to, and be responsible as a member of society

for, the physical and mental development of the population locally, nationally, and internationally;

- has a responsibility towards the natural and human-made environment in which they live, and an entitlement to a suitable environment throughout life;
- has an entitlement to a fulfilling life within and beyond their own home and to opportunities to gain a broad range of knowledge, skills and understanding, in order to become an active and informed citizen;
- has a responsibility to contribute their best endeavours to the well-being, security and personal safety of themselves, their family and the wider community.

If the school curriculum has a part to play in helping pupils to move towards achieving maturity of this kind, it seems clear that one of the cornerstones of a school's teaching needs to be Citizenship. What this might mean in practice is not creating extra slots in an already overcrowded curriculum, but a heightened awareness of where Citizenship (and the other cross-curricular themes) can be recognized as a natural part of work in the classroom. The Oxfordshire Advisory document does not advocate yet more work for teachers but a more consistently coherent approach, which identifies and makes explicit threads and links that already exist and which enhance a school's curriculum.

It is important to devise clear systems for monitoring and assessing pupil progress and involvement in initiatives to ensure that the 'broad and balanced curriculum' is really being delivered to every pupil and that the personal and social development of all is being enhanced. It is relatively easy to encourage a small band of 'good citizens' in schools, who succeed in becoming involved in their communities in positive ways; but it is much more difficult to be sure that everyone in the school is truly in training for the kind of active, participative citizenship implied in the NCC's *Guidance 8*. Indeed, it is also true that the corollary of promoting arenas in which pupils can put their point of view and be listened to, and have some influence over their present societies, can be discomforting and unsettling for the adults involved. How do the school governors feel about pupils demonstrating about the poll tax on the steps of the Town Hall, for example? Is that exercising a civic duty or fomenting civil unrest? The issues raised by 'citizenship' are likely to be comprehensive and teachers need to be prepared for that. One of the authors of this chapter well remembers the accusatory tone in the voice of an English teacher, annoyed because sixth-form students had questioned the validity of an essay title: he claimed that encouraging discussion and debate in a pastoral and social-education class was rubbing off on specific subject areas. That teacher did not have the self-confidence or willingness to allow any questioning of his methods or approaches – potentially a difficult tension within the staffroom. There needs to be consensus in each initiative about attitudes and values linked to developing citizenship awareness, and this cannot be reached without a great deal of open and full discussion.

Such discussions took place among community-link tutors and teachers from a number of schools who were involved in devising the Modular Course on Citizenship in Oxfordshire. It was developed by an LEA team of advisory and project workers, initially with the New Learning Initiative (LAPP) Project and then the Oxfordshire Achievement Project (Jones and Baglin Jones, 1992). It was compiled to achieve 'a mix of approaches and opportunities that enables the learning and development of skills, concepts, empathy, sensitivity and active knowledge through real, involving context' (Oxfordshire Achievement Project, 1989). Particular features of the course include the opportunities for learning in environments other than the classroom, and with adults other than teachers. Students are expected to exercise responsibility in real situations and to undertake tasks with real purposes and outcomes, and the emphasis is on group work, problem-solving and decision-making in both their theoretical and practical aspects. The course also provides an appropriate methodology for assessing the learning taking place – of the knowledge, understanding, skills and evaluative strategies required within the different contexts offered by the course. The practical aspects are focused on work experience, community placements, residential experience, a practical project in response to an identified need in the community, and an investigation into some aspect of provision of services in the community.

The Modular Course on Citizenship was developed so that it could be accredited through the Oxfordshire Examination Syndicate Credit Bank. The Credit Bank was an LEA initiative to support and encourage good practice in the development of modular courses in Oxfordshire schools and colleges, all of which are members of the Oxfordshire Examination Syndicate. The major focus of the Credit Bank is on modular GCSE courses, with developments taking place within a number of curriculum areas, and initially under 10 subject titles. These developments were within the parameters of the relevant National Curriculum documents, and avoiding the typical disadvantages of modular approaches, such as attempting too wide a sweep of content within a module, overassessment, and problems of curriculum coherence.

The modular Citizenship course broke new ground in that the processes of learning rather than the outcomes were to be assessed. For example, it was not only the result in terms of an essay, a work folder or a written assignment that counted towards the assessment. Equally important were the processes of preparation, application, and evaluation. Thus the course recognized the personal and individual achievements of the pupils, and thereby confirmed the active and participative nature of citizenship. It was more important to *do* citizenship than to *learn about* citizenship.

Another example of this practical and participative approach to citizenship can be seen in the exercise of mounting a Model United Nations General Assembly.

MODEL UNITED NATIONS GENERAL ASSEMBLY (MUNGA)

In 1990 the Director of the United Nations Association of Great Britain, Malcolm Harper, proposed the launching of a Model United Nations General Assembly (MUNGA) for fifth- and sixth-form students attending schools and colleges in Oxfordshire. He described it as a helpful way to introduce young pepole to the work of the United Nations and to international affairs in a structured, exciting, and participative way. This seemed to fit well with the notion of international understanding as part of the cross-curricular theme of Citizenship.

The event that resulted was county-wide, attracting some 150 pupils and students. It was organized so that teams of three pupils or students were allocated a country prior to the simulated UN meeting. On this occasion three topics were chosen – drug abuse and illicit trafficking, the destruction of the tropical rainforest, and the political situation in Kampuchea – so that one member of each country represented could become the 'expert' for the topic of the day. This required each participant to find out what policy 'their' country had on the three issues to be discussed and voted upon.

The meeting itself brought together young people from different educational establishments, and this in itself created a circumstance upon which many of the young people commented: a sharing of ideas and comments between different educational institutions. Furthermore, the fact that the President of the meeting was a representative of the United Nations Association, and that the meeting had an appointed Secretary-General, together with a Secretariat, all combined to give the occasion significance. Some delegates welcomed the opportunity to have discussions in a structured forum, and the debates about real-world issues gave an added seriousness to the occasion. For some students this was the first occasion on which they had spoken in public to a forum on a matter of substance, had been listened to seriously, and had their views given a place in the ongoing debate. It was an occasion, therefore, to learn about the United Nations, to exercise social and debating skills, and to offer comments for serious appraisal. This was added to during the afternoon session, which was attended by the Foreign Secretary, Douglas Hurd, who took a broad range of questions dealing with foreign and home affairs. For the majority of students who discussed issues with Mr Hurd, this was their first opportunity to have some form of dialogue with a real, well known politician.

The success of the occasion depended to a large degree on the amount of preparation both students and their teachers were prepared to do prior to the meeting. All the delegates were issued beforehand with a 'delegate kit' containing notes about the organization and proceedings of the United Nations Assembly, a programme for the day and a briefing for each issue. Although some teams went to great lengths (visiting embassies, using libraries, collecting information from newspapers and television, and tracking down local experts), it was possible for a team to come to some understanding of the issues using only these briefing papers.

Putting yourself in somebody else's shoes is more difficult. This aspect of the MUNGA helped pupils and students to examine other viewpoints and evaluate them – although there was a certain sympathy with the team that was allocated Iceland: 'The least satisfactory aspect of the day was having Iceland as a country, because Iceland has no real views and likes to remain neutral. We had our own views but could not voice them.' Another team member commented on the 'lively and controversial debate within working groups – although it is very difficult to defend an opinion you disagree with.' Some teams had had their preparation set as an assignment – part of a General Studies or Personal and Social Education course. There were some discrepancies, of course, in the preparedness of the teams. The students representing France, for example, unfortunately found it hard to contribute to the debate on Kampuchea. On the other hand, many teams arrived with speeches already written to be delivered to the assembly. One of the really encouraging aspects of the day was seeing many youngsters progressing from dependence on their written scripts, and growing in confidence as they challenged, and debated with, each other and the Foreign Secretary.

Three members of the organizing group agreed to act as the President, or Chairman, for the working-party groups, which discussed the three agenda topics. Specimen resolutions for debate in each group had been provided with the delegate kit. They were hotly debated, changed, redrafted or rewritten altogether by the working parties, ready for presentation to the whole assembly in the final plenary session. The three Chairmen had particular interest or expertise in their respective issues and, although there was a danger of the MUNGA being controlled by adults, it proved important for the groups to be chaired by people well used to encouraging structured debating among young people.

The teams on arrival were photographed in front of a map of the world and signed in by placing their country's name on the map. There were observers present from local United Nations branches, which provided financial support, and various members of school and LEA staff. One of the colleges of further education provided a secretariat to take notes, to encourage draft resolutions and to support the working groups. A television crew made a video and there was a stall with information and posters to publicize the work of the United Nations.

The success of this first MUNGA meeting, in many aspects beyond the issue of experiencing the work of the United Nations, prompted the idea of setting up a MUNGA meeting as an annual event. Clearly the topic issues would change from meeting to meeting but this in itself would reflect the changing challenges that face the United Nations through quite short periods of time.

The second meeting of the MUNGA was held in March 1992 in Oxfordshire, again attracting a large number of fifth- and sixth-form students from the county secondary schools and colleges of further education. On this occasion the delegates were requested to address the current UN issues of refugees, population, and the international transfer of arms. The format of the meeting and procedures followed were again those of the initial meeting and reflected the way the United Nations organization went about its business. All delegates had been provided with a briefing sheet on the rules of procedure of the General Assembly. Each delegate also received a copy of a letter sent by Lord Richard, QC, Vice-Chairman of the United Nations Association. Additionally, all delegates received from the United Kingdom Director, Malcolm Harper, a letter of information on the work of the UN, how to go about preparing themselves for the MUNGA experience, what could be achieved in gaining advance knowledge on the subjects to be debated, and how to handle views of 'delegate countries' that might not be the views of the delegates personally. The delegate-students were reminded that it was not only the views of the superpowers that were essential to the effective working of the UN organizations: all countries, through their delegates, had the opportunities to offer opinions at the UN meeting, to organize and negotiate in caucus and to draft amendments to the resolutions. Students were all urged to be active participants in the simulation exercise, to make speeches and comments, and to ask questions. In both the 1990 and 1992 events, this was an urging that required no reinforcement on the day.

The delegate kit also included a United Nations press release sent out by the UN to give information about member nations. Delegates were encouraged to approach embassies in this country for information about policies, and they received a list of questions to help them in these or other enquiries. It has been found that delegates themselves, following a MUNGA meeting, want to participate or obtain further information about the UN organization in Britain. To this end all delegates were provided with lists of addresses, not only in relation to the UN, but for such organizations as the British Refugee Council, Friends of the Earth and Oxfam. Additional handouts were also available at the meeting, particularly related to the three topics under discussion but also on a wide range of topics that would be of interest to someone interested and active regarding citizenship matters. Delegates also received an invitation to attend a meeting of the United Nations Association's Conference on the Environment and Development. The purpose of this meeting was to canvass the views of people in the Oxfordshire area about ways to halt and reverse the effects of environmental degradation, while increasing efforts to promote sustainable and environmentally sound development in all countries. A direct purpose of this meeting was to send a resolution to the United Nations Earth Summit conference to be held in Rio de Janeiro in June 1992.

An additional feature of this second MUNGA meeting was the opportunity for certain delegates to participate in an emergency debate of the Security Council to consider the fact that Resolution 660, concerning the invasion of Kuwait by Iraq, was not being implemented. This meeting was open only to those delegates who represented nations who were members of the Security Council.

CONCLUSION

In this chapter we have outlined some of the positive approaches and developments in the area of Citizenship studies in Oxfordshire. Several of them need more time to ripen into agreed and accepted practices but what is important is the growing awareness and excitement of teachers who are acknowledging and making explicit their contributions to the creation of tomorrow's citizens.

REFERENCES

Cheer, S (1991) *The Junior Citizen of Banbury Initiative*, MA thesis, Leicester University.

Jones, N and Baglin Jones, E (1992) *Learning to Behave: Curriculum and Whole-School Management Approaches*, London: Kogan Page.

Oxfordshire Achievement Project (1989) *Citizenship: A Modular Course*, Wheatley: Oxfordshire County Council.

Speaker's Commission on Citizenship (1990) *Encouraging Citizenship*, London: HMSO.

Chapter 10

Rights, Responsibilities and School Ethos

Jeremy Cunningham

INTRODUCTION

In education, we are playing the long game. It usually takes a year or two after our training as secondary teachers for us to realize that we are teachers of children, not subjects. It takes most of us rather longer to become aware that the actions we take every day in school have a persistent impact over a lifetime. The life-lessons learnt at the age of 13 will be played out by the grandparent 50 years later.

Citizenship education derives some of its urgency from a realization that democratic values are not historically inevitable but have to be nurtured, maintained and defended. The stirring events in Eastern Europe should not blind us to the fact that throughout the continent many young people are attracted to simplistic and extremist political creeds. Schools have a vital part to play in the transmission of the basic moral and political values of our society and a curriculum made up of subjects divorced from a moral framework will not serve this purpose.

Those who framed the National Curriculum did not at first seem to understand the importance of citizenship and political literacy; but the (anonymous) NCC document *Education for Citizenship* (NCC, 1990) has incorporated some of the important insights achieved by thinkers in the field. While using the well-known categories of 'knowledge and understanding', 'skills', 'attitudes' and 'values', the document acknowledges that citizenship is developed through the hidden curriculum, the whole atmosphere and ethos of the community and of the school within it. In other words it is nonsense to aim to develop moral autonomy and democratic values within a rigidly authoritarian structure, and self-defeating to expect future citizens to deal fairly with the duties and rights of others unless they have experienced a model of a just society, or a determined attempt to portray one.

It is quite common to read about the importance of school ethos but rare to be given examples of schools achieving a good one. This is my excuse for an account of policies and practice at Carterton Community College, which are intended to create a fair and happy school, and one that fosters good citizenship through its normal procedures and traditions. They are the result of almost daily discussion over many years, and no individuals can take credit for their development or blame for their failures. Not everything here is a glowing account of success. If we are going to try out new ideas we have to be ready to learn from our mistakes and our weaknesses. I have no doubt that large numbers of schools have developed their own equivalent systems and procedures, and this contribution stands for all those who have realized that knowledge must be unlocked in a moral framework. It is never totally value-free.

THE MORAL FRAMEWORK

It is clear that we no longer live in a society where all Christian values are accepted by everyone, and yet many people are concerned that their children should have a good moral education. Even if they are not themselves Christian, large numbers of parents are happy for their children to go to church schools because of the strong sense of moral commitment.

State schools have often found themselves in a kind of vacuum, for where the teachers themselves are not uniformly religious, they feel it is hypocritical to support the forms of a religious and moral structure in which they do not believe. The students, too, resent an undiluted diet of religious moral instruction. The variety of cultural backgrounds and faiths appears to make the task of maintaining a universal morality within a school very difficult. One response has been to abandon the public and corporate expression of values by reducing or even eliminating school assemblies and other similar events or celebrations. This is an understandable but unhelpful response, for the school assembly provides a powerful opportunity for the reinforcement of collective values. The 1988 Act has done nothing to resolve this problem, but anachronistically has insisted on a national religious approach that almost amounts to government-supported indoctrination. Those who cannot accept this instruction continue quietly to ignore the law, but sometimes are at a loss for a convincing and embracing moral framework. What are our collective values? Why are some things right and others wrong when one does not depend on religious principles?

The concepts of human rights and responsibilities provide a wider moral foundation than any purely religious scheme, and yet they include the tolerance of different faiths and the respect for the spiritual element of life. Rights and responsibilities provide the type of framework that so many teachers have felt to be lacking where religious values are in decline. They also include the essential political elements of democracy and justice, which cannot just be assumed to be absorbed by our young people but have to be fostered and developed. It is in this political field that the 1988 Act has shown itself to be more feeble, relying on traditional History and Geography to educate future citizens in the processes of their own present-day society.

It is one of the great failures of the 1988 Act that the government did not recognize that human-rights education provides a foundation for moral values and justification for political literacy without falling into the trap of endorsing religious or political indoctrination. The National Curriculum Council's advice on citizenship is an attempt to remedy this failure, but does not have the strength of the law behind it.

It is the premise of this chapter that education for rights and responsibilities is the essential element of what the National Curriculum Council terms 'Citizenship', and that it includes not only knowledge about rights and responsibilities but their daily practice as part of the declared policy and ethos of the school.

EDUCATION FOR RIGHTS AND RESPONSIBILITIES

Education for human rights has to begin with young people's sense of fairness. Piaget's study of the moral development of children, carried out with Swiss children in the 1920s, found that those children had a well-developed sense of justice and fair play, based on the culture of the playground (Piaget, 1972). One wonders whether the same is true of children raised in the late-20th-century European urban environment, watching an average of 30 hours' television a week and with access to 'adult' videos. Even the moral stance of cartoons and crime-thrillers has changed and there is a much more hazy approach to good and evil. All the same, most children care passionately about fair treatment for themselves and their immediate circle. Childhood solidarity still holds, although adults are less ready to discourage young people from 'tale-telling', in response to a heightened consciousness of bullying.

Another key concept for adolescents is hypocrisy. The healthy emerging adult personality is constantly judging the injunctions of parents and other authorities for their rational basis and for their consistency. First, what are the reasons for making that rule, or for telling me to do that? Second, do those who make these rules live by them themselves? Schools, with their systems and codes, their rules and resulting infractions, are arenas in which young people test out the society they are joining. Therefore it is essential that a school should have a rational and consistent approach to justice, fairness, rights, duties, the resolution of disputes and infractions of codes of behaviour.

We have all encountered a few individuals who believe that the students are the opposition and that rule-breaking must be dealt with quickly and with no hesitation. The principle that it doesn't matter whether the person punished is guilty or not, because he or she has probably done something just as bad, is employed as a kind of catch-all. The assumption remains that the real business of the school is the transmission of knowledge and not much else. It is too costly in time to take the trouble to establish the facts, to listen to witnesses, to give the accused an opportunity to speak up for themselves.

The real business of the school is the transmission of knowledge and culture, *and* the assistance of the development of autonomous individuals with a moral approach to life. People learn this approach through example and through the opportunity to engage in the rational discussion of issues and dilemmas. Paramount among these dilemmas is the issue of conflict of rights: more simply – one person's fairness may be another person's unfairness.

Let us move for a moment from the school to review how human rights are incorporated in national and international law.

It is a feature of British law that rights do not exist as codified principles: we are allowed to do anything that the law does not prohibit. Many people think there should be a comprehensive Bill of Rights to bring us into line with the international treaties that we have ratified. The most significant international documents are:

- The Universal Declaration of Human Rights, 1948. An internationally endorsed set of principles, with moral force but without the force of law.
- The European Convention of Human Rights, 1950. A collective guarantee at a European level of a number of the principles in the Universal Declaration, supported by international judicial machinery that must be respected by contracting states. It is not a substitute for national guarantees of fundamental rights but is supplementary to them, and proceedings cannot be instituted until after all domestic remedies have been exhausted. The convention has been ratified by all 21 members of the Council of Europe.
- The UN International Covenants on Human Rights, 1976. These are treaty provisions that establish legal obligations on the part of each ratifying state. There are two covenants: one dealing with civil and political rights and the other with economic and social rights.
- The UN Convention on the Rights of the Child, 1989. When 20 nations have ratified this convention it will have the force of an international treaty, and will be a powerful framework for protecting children's rights and ensuring greater participation by children in deciding their future. The United Kingdom is a signatory but has not yet ratified it.

SIGNIFICANT PROVISIONS FOR DAILY LIFE IN A SECONDARY SCHOOL

Education itself is a vital human right, and all the documents naturally underline the importance of ensuring that citizens know what their rights and responsibilities are, and that they are educated in the spirit and practice of human rights. There are a number of provisions that have special relevance for the daily life of a secondary school. First, from those that are already in force and that were designed primarily for adults:

- No one shall be subjected to degrading treatment or punishment.
- Everyone shall be presumed innocent until proved guilty.
- Everyone has the right to be informed of the nature and cause of an accusation.
- Everyone is entitled to a fair hearing.
- Everyone has the right to respect for his private and family life, his home and his correspondence.
- Everyone has the right to freedom of thought, conscience and religion, subject only to those limitations necessary in a democratic society to protect public safety or for the protection of the rights and freedoms of others.
- Everyone has the right to freedom of expression and assembly. These carry the duties and responsibilities of prevention of disorder and crime, and protection of public health, of morals, and of the public reputation of others.
- Any advocacy of national, racial or religious hatred that incites discrimination or violence shall be prohibited.
- Every citizen has the right to take part in the conduct of public affairs, to vote at genuine periodic elections, by universal and equal suffrage, and by secret ballot.
- All persons are equal before the law and are entitled to rights and freedoms without discrimination on any ground such as race, colour, sex, language, religion, political or other opinion, national or social origin, property, birth or other status.
- Persons belonging to ethnic, religious or linguistic minorities have the right to enjoy their own culture, practise their own religion and use their own language.
- Nothing in this list may be interpreted as implying for any state, group or person any right to engage in any activity . . . aimed at the destruction of any of these rights and freedoms.

The Convention on the Rights of the Child is particularly important in ensuring that children are entitled to the same basic rights as adults, with exceptions allowed only to respect the rights or reputations of others, or for reasons of national security, public order, public health or morals. Some of the most significant provisions are:

- The best interests of the child should be the primary consideration in all actions.
- Children have a right to freedom of expression, thought, conscience and religion. They have a right to peaceful assembly.
- Children should not be subjected to unlawful interference with privacy, family, home or correspondence, nor to attacks on honour and reputation.
- Disabled children have a right to special care, education and training designed to help them achieve the greatest possible self-reliance.
- School discipline must be administered in a manner consistent with the child's human dignity and with the Convention.
- Education should be directed at developing the child's personality and talents, fostering respect for basic human rights and developing respect for the child's own cultural and national values and those of others.

It is possible to object to this type of list by noting the absence of the word 'duty'. The language of rights seems to be defensive rather than positive. Yet the duty consists of respecting the rights of others, and of approaching conflicts of interest in a rational and a fair manner, rather than according to power, violence or brute force. The world shows us that rationality and freedom have to be struggled for, and that 'duty' is often used by repressive powers determined to maintain themselves. That is not to say that it is a redundant word, merely that it is the other side of the coin: for example, the right to enjoy one's own culture means the duty to respect the culture of others. A school will be unlikely to use the exact, legalistic language of human-rights documents in framing its policies, but will seek to use the everyday language of fairness, responsibilities and rights. Nevertheless it is clear that, according to the conventions described above, schools have a duty under international law to ensure that students know about their own rights and responsibilities. It is intriguing to speculate about the number of British schools failing in this respect.

CARTERTON COMMUNITY COLLEGE PRINCIPLES AND CODE OF CONDUCT

Carterton Community College serves a town of some 15,000 people in West Oxfordshire. The character of the community is strongly influenced by the presence of RAF Brize Norton, the largest RAF base in the country. The partnership of four primary schools and the

Community College has to deal with a very high turnover rate, well over 10% per year, caused by service postings. The Community College incorporates 11–16 education for about 450 students, a preschool playgroup and crèche, and a community education programme, under a unified management structure. At 16, over 60% of students continue in education or training in nearby school sixth forms or at the West Oxfordshire College.

The framing and reviewing of codes and sets of principles is important more for the process involved than for the resulting structures. We have not recently invested in this area of community-college work, but when we find that we need clarity about points of principle, we have a structure to work to. Close analysis of our principles, for example, reveals no mention of the word 'peace', and yet it is an essential foundation of our daily life. Should we rewrite the principles or do we need to only when peace or lack of it becomes an issue or major problem?

Here are three sections from the principles:

Education of the whole person
Our aim is to help each person develop their whole potential – body, mind, emotions and spiritual life. We are determined that all people should have a fair chance to do well, regardless of background, race, sex, disability or age. . . . We believe that successful personal development means good learning.

Fairness
A happy school is good for learning. People treat each other fairly and in a friendly professional way. Respect is given to adults for their experience and their commitment to helping the young. Respect is given to students for their hard work and cooperation.

Care for the environment
We care for our land and buildings and the natural world around us. We recognize the hard work that goes into building a school and maintaining its grounds and facilities. We keep our site tidy, repair it and improve it.

The process of revision of the principles and code of conduct involves students, staff, parents and governors through open discussion and negotiation. At class level, students are encouraged to play their part in framing rules for a successful learning atmosphere, and the approach can be used in the wider context. It is not necessary to refer to human-rights documents in detail for this process to be in harmony with the fundamental principles outlined above.

DISPUTES AND DISCIPLINE

The way in which we set about resolving disputes and dealing with infractions of school principles and code of conduct is intended to be an education in human rights and responsibilities. The essential principle is that disputes should not be seen simply as irritating interruptions to the essential business of the school and therefore to be dealt with as quickly as possible, but a means by which we can express moral values, nurture effective moral development and promote respect for rights and responsibilities.

Lawrence Kohlberg (1971) suggests that people pass through stages of moral understanding and that their passage to a higher stage is made possible by hearing the rational arguments of those who have reached it. Having to resolve dilemmas or confront conflicts of interest accelerates moral growth. It is possible for growth to be arrested, and many people stop at what Kohlberg terms the 'law-and-order orientation', which is a rigid and narrow respect for fixed, codified rules, without a corresponding understanding of what the rules are for.

This can be observed in those who are very concerned with the letter of the law, who want a detailed list of rules so that they can know exactly where they stand on every issue (and what they can get away with without technically breaking the rules). What is essential for people who are at this stage is to hear the reasons why one person's right may conflict with another's, or why a particular freedom carries obligations with it. It is even more effective if the individual hears the reasons from a peer rather than from someone in authority.

Another of Kohlberg's insights is that people are not usually receptive to the methods of moral thinking associated with stages much higher than their existing one. For example, a relatively early moral stage is the 'good boy' stage, at which the individual is carrying out the right action simply for adult or peer approval. Before real moral autonomy can be reached, the person has to go through a stage of understanding the concept of rules and codes as coherent systems.

It is asking a great deal that before we handle any case we should know the precise stage of moral development of any individual, but it is possible to set up procedures that will aid the development of moral thinking, on the part of adults and students. In other words the school has to have its own *due process* for the resolution of problems and disputes.

The traditional discipline model is that of investigation, judgement, sanction. Teachers are often investigators, interrogators, judges, counsellors and punitive authorities all rolled into one. The potential for miscarriage of justice is relatively high, especially where young adults without a fully worked-out moral stance of their own are dealing with complex disputes between individuals, or incidents of aggression. The experience of being punished unfairly is a devastating one and nearly every adult can vividly remember such incidents from their own schooldays. The antipathy to the system, to the school, to adults in general that even one incident can create is deeply destructive to education. Furthermore, individuals who have been treating others badly or aggressively provide themselves with their own distorted justification if they are punished without full consideration of the facts or evidence. Then, instead of the problem being solved or peace being achieved, there begins a new cycle of anger or aggression.

The system we try to follow at Carterton Community College is investigation, resolution, restitution, sanction, and communication. Through it we aim to act out human-rights principles in the solution of problems and the handling of misdemeanours.

Investigation

The essential principle is 'everyone is presumed innocent until proven guilty'. It is striking how often 'evidence' turns out to be hearsay or impression. The first step is to assemble the facts carefully. In interpersonal disputes or cases of aggression it is useful to take written notes to clarify essential points of difference. Students can be asked to name someone they would trust to be a fair witness – not a close personal friend – and the accounts of witnesses can be combined. We have found this particularly useful where an aggressive student flatly denies hurting someone. The independent nature of the witnesses is central to the task of ensuring that the aggressor (and their family in serious cases) accepts that they have done wrong.

When investigating the causes of a fight between students we always allow a cooling-off period first. A physically injured party is not necessarily guiltless. The person seen to inflict a blow may not be the only guilty party. Sometimes fights are caused by manipulators who 'wind up' people with a sense of grievance by reporting nonexistent threats. Who is then the more to blame, those who break the peace or those who manipulated them? Sometimes a blow is a last desperate resort after weeks of mental pressure or name-calling.

We always write notes of statements and read them back to the individuals. They can be kept in the student records and are essential for future reference. Anger is not shown towards a suspect and we recognize that people under pressure occasionally make false confessions, so we have to be careful about using threats.

The most difficult type of incident to deal with is a dispute between a teacher and a student in which each presents a different picture of the event. In deference to the teacher's professional position, it is correct for a senior member of staff to interview the teacher first, but that will appear small compensation to an aggrieved colleague who is looking for support. Yet we teachers are not perfect and occasionally we do make mistakes. The best among us have the capacity to recognize that and even to apologize to our students. It should not appear to be lack of support that a dispute should be properly investigated. A student's word can be given a value that will be in relation to their past history of honesty, cooperation and fair treatment of others. Some teachers will find it unacceptable to go as far as listening to the student, feeling that that means taking the student's side, so it is important to explain the role of due process in moral education.

Resolution

Resolution means the acceptance of the problem by all parties as finished and solved. It is an important step because it keeps attention on the problem, its causes and how to avoid it, instead of on a mechanical approach to justice. It also prevents the issue from just fading away. In a dispute between students a compromise or apology may lead to each party being asked if they are satisfied that the matter is resolved; if they are, a symbolic gesture like a handshake or a written statement about future intentions sets the seal on the agreement. We must remember that students have very little privacy in schools, and little chance of solving problems on their own. There are always too many people wanting to become involved or even to stir things up. Some private time is very useful for most people. They can make peace in their own way and such a peace is more likely to last.

If the problem recurs, the adult who invested the time in solving it becomes the injured party, and it should always be made clear to students that, although it is our job to help solve disputes, the main business of the school is learning: teachers' time is valuable and should be at the service of *all* students. Any dispute needing teacher intervention uses up much valuable time.

In the case of a serious offence against the school code, other people's rights will have been violated – for example, the right to property and the right to peacefully pursue one's studies – for the code is designed to encourage responsibility and to protect the rights of all. It is essential to explain the connection between the offence and fairness to others. For example, a student disrupting a lesson is trampling on the other students' right to learn – it is not fair. Offenders cannot give back the lost learning, but the first step is to recognize in what way they have been unfair.

Resolution can be connected to a contract. To be worthy of the name, a contract has to be freely entered into, and its terms explained very clearly and written down. One advantage of a contract is the provision of short-term concrete goals with a directly connected pay-off. It is useful for people at a relatively low level of moral development who can respond to an instrumental/behaviourist approach. For example, a student who has been disruptive can earn points on a report card for every successful lesson. At the end of a defined period a certain number of points can earn a particular privilege. This works well with close parental involvement, for there may be more opportunities for reward in the family context. It is essential for the student to be party to the reasoning behind a contract, as the essential process is that of self-knowledge.

Restitution

Restitution means paying back, or making amends, for injury. The term 'making amends' is a useful one because of its suggestion of mending. Something has been broken – trust or peace or someone's learning – but perhaps it can be mended. It is possible to pay back for property damage, but it is not easy to make direct reparation for physical or mental suffering. The school has to act as an intermediary and receive reparation on the injured party's behalf. Not only that but an offence against the school code is a blow to the self-respect and morale of the community. It will have cost precious energy, time and good will. It is perfectly fair to expect an offender to pay something back through some activity useful to the school or wider community. The offender, too, has the chance to gain self-respect, the lack of which is so frequent a cause of the problem in the first place.

We always aim to place long-term moral growth above the desire for punishment, but people are not happy if community service appears to be a reward or privilege instead of a punishment. As in the wider world, reform comes into conflict with revenge. It is in our nature to notice our failures rather than our successes, but by keeping careful records of decisions we can analyse the effectiveness of our various methods. The advantage of this approach is that after a misdemeanour the offender is reintegrated into the community and benefits from its normal warmth and support. Positive reinforcement and affection work much better in the long run than punishment and dislike.

Sanctions

'No one shall be subjected to . . . degrading treatment or punishment' (Article 3, European Convention). The finding of the European Court that corporal punishment in schools amounts to 'degrading' treatment had immediate effects on state schools in this country, as we have ratified the European Convention on Human Rights. Meaningless tasks, personal indignity, public humiliation, sarcastic remarks could all be interpreted as degrading treatment. Any treatment that demeans the individual also demeans the institution.

Sanctions are the symbol of the community's determination not to tolerate particular infringements of its code. They are designed to give warning to potential offenders and to deter them from offending. The ultimate sanction is exclusion from the community, temporary or permanent. English education law has complex and definite procedures designed to protect the interests of student, parents, staff, governors and education authorities. It is seen as a last resort, for it deprives the student of a full education until alternative provision can be made.

Our policy is to create an ethos where objectively mild sanctions, such as withdrawal of privileges, are treated with the utmost seriousness of purpose and are seldom used. The law of diminishing returns applies to any sanctions that are overused, however severe they seem at first. The views of parents and families are very important, for people have their own views of how serious an offence may be. For example some people think that fighting is a normal part of growing up and are amazed when we take a serious view of violence. Parents may wish to impose their own punishment, which may or may not be more severe than that imposed at school. Open and easy relationships with parents allow matters to be thoroughly discussed, and the double-jeopardy rule – that no one should be punished twice for the same offence – can be applied. It is usually possible to work out a joint approach with the family, but only (as noted above) if they are absolutely sure about the facts and the justice of the case.

We are a small community, in which individuals are very well known, and there can be no system of fixed penalties. Previous records are always available, and the student's personal profile, which includes a wide range of achievements and successes, should always be consulted before making a decision. To treat each individual as a cipher or a blank page is the antithesis of equal treatment. Sometimes young people do not appreciate this point and compare their treatment with others', so it is essential to explain that *equal* treatment does not mean the *same* treatment.

Communication

One of the weaknesses of a large centralized system of justice is that the machine seems to operate without reference to the individuals for whose benefit it is intended. It is quite common for a victim of crime not to be informed when suspects are apprehended, when a court case is called or when a sentence is given. At Carterton we can take advantage of our smallness of scale to ensure that good communication maintains the ethos and respect for the code. First, any injured party must not be forgotten in our zeal to apprehend the offender and put him or her on the right track. Anyone who has suffered needs the reassurance that we are working for them, not just applying some abstract system of justice. We try to ensure that they play their part in the resolution of the matter and that they receive any reparation due to them. Attention to detail here is repaid by the respect they give the community college in return and therefore lessens the likelihood of their offending at a later date. On the other hand, people who have felt abandoned are more likely to say to themselves, 'When I had a problem nobody cared for me, why should I care for anyone else?' This attitude lies behind the process by which those who were bullied when young and small sometimes turn into bullies when they are older.

Parents are key figures here too. They do not always receive a clear picture from their children and they can have the impression that no one is bothering to do anything. We have to be honest about our inability to solve everything, but the essential message is that we will try our best. On the other hand, parents of offenders do not always accept that we are taking the right course, and need open and frank discussion about the reasons for our actions.

It is sometimes tempting to deal with a matter by promising immunity from parental involvement in return for information or a confession. This is a dangerous path to follow as it violates parental rights. Only in minor cases, or in extreme cases such as suspected child abuse, can it be justifiable to withhold information. It is particularly important to maintain files that can be opened to parents. In some countries, such as the USA and Canada, parents have the legal right to see all files kept on their children. In Britain, the Data Protection Act of 1984 does not apply to non-computer files; nevertheless, there are good grounds for supporting the principle of open files. School reports often play an important role in juvenile court proceedings and it is quite possible for general statements of opinion based on scanty factual evidence to find their way onto school files. Statements of opinion about parents are not relevant matters for recording.

We have learned that communication is vital, too, for staff and students. When a discipline matter is handed over from junior to senior staff, it is all too easy to forget to communicate about what has happened and why. Thorough notes are essential, so that the tutor can see the process of resolution and/or sanction. Ideally the tutor remains involved all the way through, because he or she will be the one responsible for the student when the process is complete. This also provides a useful method of in-service training for less experienced members of staff. Actions taken with full knowledge of the facts and previous record may not seem correct to those who have a scanty knowledge of the matter, just as newspaper reports of trials and sentences do not give readers the level of information available to jury and judge. It is not possible to give all staff and students the full details of every incident, and therefore the gradual development of a joint approach with a common sense of purpose is absolutely essential.

DEMOCRATIC SKILLS

Is our school council (called a parliament) just a talk shop? We don't
think so. It has a good record of pushing for and achieving improve-
ments in the quality of life for students. One area has been the provision
of lockers for students. This was taken up by the parliament and
approaches were made to the Parents/Teachers/Friends Association,
which funded their installation and did a lot of the labour as well. The
parliament has raised money for charities, and consulted with all
students over the destination of the funds that were raised. As an
example, parliament voted funds to support improved equipment for a
local special school with which we have close links.

Parliament took on the issue of uniform changes, specifically trousers
and culottes for girls. As a result of a parliament resolution, the parents
and staff were balloted and a modified uniform was tried out and finally
accepted. Carterton has no head boy or head girl. The chair and
secretary of the parliament represent the community college on formal
occasions or with important visitors. Each tutor group elects two
representatives, using its own voting system. (The parliament recommends but does not enforce secret ballots.) Officers are elected yearly
by secret ballot. There is no rule that the chair has to be in the top year.

The basic skills of classroom discussion are the foundation of all
democracy. If people can listen to each other with respect and tolerance
and can develop their own powers of argument, everything else will
follow. In Britain we are the victims of the adversarial approach, which
in the formal debate gives the process of the duel a higher value than the
mutual search for truth. Trials, the parliamentary system, television
debates and interviews tend to follow this pattern, and students with
developing egos and a healthy competitive instinct are always ready to
copy it. Individuals have to be trained how to listen to each other and to
respect each other's opinions. How often the quiet speaker, the
unconfident individual, or the unpopular one can have their views
squashed by the majority, unless the teacher is very experienced at
handling the whole class discussion. And yet unless people are used to
frank and open debate at class level they are unlikely to have the chance
to perform in a wider forum. Personal health and social education
(PHSE) programmes such as 'Skills for Adolescence' have had an impact
on our readiness to negotiate classroom rules with the students, but the
teacher needs a firm authority to be able to protect the rights of each
individual in the class. At Carterton we certainly have not achieved this
goal and we need to train ourselves in more sophisticated chairing skills.
The 'discussion' between teacher and students sitting in straight rows
is still common, and quite simple analysis shows that in any such class
a very few students monopolize the air time.

CEREMONIES AND RITES OF PASSAGE

Many state schools have shied away from ceremonies and rituals, believing that they foster elitism and division. Public celebration and praise are very important features of the community college. Every effort is made to spread the net widely so that nearly everyone is recognized in one way or another. This is done by praising or rewarding whole groups and by ensuring that prizes are not monopolized by a small group of individuals. The annual Awards Evening is designed to be both formal and friendly, on a human scale, with music, drama excerpts and a visiting speaker. In a small school it is possible to hand out all the examination certificates individually. We make much of the presentation of completed Records of Achievement, which the students have been working on throughout their career. This is best done at the valedictory service, just before GCSE exams begin, and when the Year 11 students are about to begin study leave. The service always has a warm atmosphere and usually includes some performances by leaving students. It is followed by a buffet lunch prepared jointly by students and staff, to which the students invite a few guests. A notable event is the Year 11 dinner dance, held just before Christmas, a formal event with speakers and guests. The Year 10 students serve their elders and do all the cooking and washing-up. The following year they are the participants.

The effect of events like these, and the parties that follow them, is to build on the excellent daily relationships between staff and students. The opportunities to work together in planning and carrying them out, and to compliment everyone afterwards, help maintain a positive atmosphere, which is able to absorb the occasional crisis. One secret of their success has been the outstanding master-of-ceremonies skills of the Deputy Head, who manages to link services, celebrations, and events with an amusing, personal and distinctly unpompous style.

We have not managed to achieve the right balance with our assembly programme. Carterton has three assemblies each week, divided into upper and lower school, with a regular and comprehensive programme of visiting clergy. There is no doubt that the assemblies are mainly of a Christian character, but we have not managed to build in a coherent approach to other faiths or types of belief. Carterton does not have a wide range of ethnic groups, and although the service families have travelled, it is within a very protected and limited environment. The students are asking to hear from a wider range of people, partly as a result of some of the community/RE work they have experienced in the curriculum. Assemblies are a vehicle for conveying information about human rights, and the right forum for putting into practice the principle of freedom of conscience. Our task is to broaden the range of principles

and world views that are propounded by our visitors and yet to remain
true to the traditions of our native culture.

COMMUNITY SERVICE AND RESPONSIBILITIES

The Community College motto is 'Service before Self' and consistent
efforts have been made to live up to it. For many years Age Concern
was based in a room on-site and students contributed their time to the
elderly members. A recent development has been the weekly visit of
secondary-age pupils from a local special school. These youngsters have
multiple disabilities. Carterton students help care for them and make
them part of the daily routine. We have found that students in trouble
because of a low self-image and the lack of opportunities for responsibility can do extremely well when faced with the challenge of looking
after others. Such arrangements are made with great care in order to
avoid the sense of exploiting our visitors for our own ends, but in fact
it makes for a good relationship that each partner has something to
offer and something to gain.

The playgroup and crèches also provide opportunities for work
experience and responsibilities, not only as part of the curriculum, but
also for volunteer work. A further idea for community service on the
site itself is the environment. Students have gained self-respect and
confidence by looking after small livestock, wild-flower gardens, ponds
and nature reserves. Volunteers have started up can-recycling projects,
and the routine clearing of litter is taken as a matter of course. The
importance of a well-loved environment cannot be overestimated: time
and again staff and students comment on how attractice the site is and
how that helps them feel positive about their work. It is an excellent
result of local management that it is possible to invest quite small sums
in the environment for outstanding results.

Another area of responsibility is the reception system. Each student
in years 7 to 9 spends two separate half-days on the main reception desk
by the front entrance, signing in visitors and directing them. When
visitors ask for a tour of the community college, the receptionist may
well be asked to show them around.

None of these ideas is unique, and we have picked up many of them
from other schools, but we are constantly seeking more opportunities
for community service and responsibility. It is the staff view that many
more students could benefit from increased responsibilities. The
students themselves are positive about anything that has a clear benefit
to others, such as raising money for charities, or caring for a particular
area of the school, like the drama studio or music block. There have
been attempts to link older students with younger tutor groups as 'older
brothers and sisters'. These have been arranged on an ad-hoc basis

where there have been bullying problems, but there has been no formal organized scheme. It is my view that students could do much more to clean up their own workplace. The lesson that someone else is there to clean up after you is not a good one.

A major area of failure is in the routine sharing of organizational tasks. When a room has to be cleared at the end of a disco or event, the positive and the energetic are there as usual, adults as well as youngsters. We have not really tackled the question of how to engage a much larger group, who by working together could complete the task in a fraction of the time. After a recent farewell dinner for a member of staff, the cook was left to clear and wash up with help from a fraction of those colleagues who attended and enjoyed the evening. The assumption that everyone can imagine, or remember, what work has to be done does not hold good. We all have an unfair habit of forgetting those who work behind the scenes, and the load continues to fall on the 'givers'. Community service could begin at home, with a greater equality in the sharing of tasks.

THE CURRICULUM

It is not the purpose of this chapter to give a detailed view on the place of human rights and responsibilities in the curriculum. Suffice it to say that the present structure of the National Curriculum pays no more than lip-service to the necessity for understanding and knowledge in this field. It is obvious that if people are to understand their rights and duties, time has to be allocated to this study. It is equally clear that the Geography and History Orders go no way to meeting this need and the vague reference to the 'social sciences' in the Citizenship document suggests an optional subject, somehow fitted in on top of all the core and foundation subjects. It is ironic to compare the furore over what precise history content should be studied by all our citizens – for instance the Romans, their administration and their law – with the silence over fundamental human rights. Is it not important for all students to be introduced to the present law and political system of their own country and to those aspects of international law to which we are bound?

We have found it just possible to include a course on the law and rights and responsibilities within the framework of an Integrated Humanities GCSE course followed by all students. The course includes a routine visit to a trial at Oxford Crown Court, visits from police and probation officers, some detailed work on capital punishment and an introduction to the concept and the conventions of human rights. The Universal Declaration is studied in simplified language. The Northern Examining Association operates a Law in Society (Rights and Duties)

GCSE course that is an excellent vehicle for this kind of work, but we do not have the curriculum space to fit it in.

The PHSE programme provides opportunities for general citizenship work, but the pressure on this programme is intense, as it carries much of the burden of careers education, sex education, road safety, first aid and so on. For the time being, then, the main plank of our platform remains the whole-institution approach, with a relatively slender support in the main curriculum. I would estimate that this is the position in the vast majority of English secondary schools. It is absolutely clear that appeals for a cross-curricular approach to five or six different themes or dimensions will be unheard unless there is a solid section of the mainstream subject curriculum for them to be based on. The hope that by diligent planning and cross-referencing everything necessary will be covered by every student is unrealistic.

CONCLUSION

We face the immense challenge of raising educational expectations and standards. Conscientious teachers everywhere are facing up to the issue of motivation and the effective school. All are agreed that motivation and morale depend on mutually agreed values, a common purpose, open and fair relationships, good leadership and communication. Furthermore, the lessons from Europe as a whole are that we have to work consciously and explicitly to maintain a culture of tolerance, fairness and participation. What seems to have been missing in England has been an explicit value system that is not a rigid code, a religious or political imperative, but a flexible, durable and global consensus capable of containing within itself a huge variety of cultures and beliefs. How do you explain to yourself and to your students why you are doing the job? What do you refer to when you consider the long-term implications of being an educator, not just the short-term goals of this or that examination? The students themselves want something to test themselves against, and the parents are prepared to back a religious stand for the moral integrity it offers, even if they are not themselves religious.

I believe that rights and responsibilities provide a moral framework for society in general and the school in particular, and our daily work can reflect the fundamental global values enshrined in the human-rights conventions of our time. This does not mean an uncritical acceptance of every element, for rights and duties conflict at every point, but an understanding of the essence of justice and hope.

As a postscript I offer a story told by Claudio Magris (1990) in his book *Danube*, as he remembers a teacher of German called Trani who had a strong impact on him.

To that man, the butt of so many criticisms at the Parents' Meetings,

I owe not only my discovery of Central European culture, but also one of the most important and unusual lessons in morality. If it is true that he trafficked in private lessons, then he was unable to practise strict justice himself, but to us he taught the sense of what is right and contempt for what is wrong. Like so many classes, our class had its victim, a fat, very timorous lad who blushed and sweated at the drop of a hat, who was unable to trade insults and was the object of that unwitting but no less blameworthy cruelty that we all have in us; cruelty which, if not kept at bay by some precise law imposed from within or without, will flare up in spite of ourselves to the detriment of whoever is weak at that moment.

Not one of us was innocent in this regard, and none of us was aware of being guilty. One day, while with theatrical gestures Trani was teaching us the conjugation of the German strong verbs, this boy's next-door neighbour, by the name of Sandrin, suddenly seized his fountain pen and snapped it in half. I can still see the victim's face as it grew red and sweaty, and his eyes filling with tears at the injustice of it, and his awareness that he was incapable of putting up a fight. When the teacher asked him why he had done that, Sandrin answered, 'I felt nervous . . . and when I'm nervous I can't control myself . . . I'm just made like this, it's my nature.' To our astonishment – and to the delight of the aggressor and greater humiliation of the offended party – Trani replied: 'I understand. You couldn't do anything else, you're just made that way, it's your nature. We can't blame you, it's just life, that's all. . . .' And he went on with the lesson.

A quarter of an hour later he began to complain about the fug, to loosen his tie and unbutton his waistcoat, to open the window and slam it shut again, to tell us that his nerves were on edge until, feigning a sudden fit of rage, he seized hold of Sandrin's pens, pencils and notebooks, snapped them and ripped them and threw them all over the place. Then affecting to grow calm, he said to Sandrin: 'I'm so sorry, dear boy, I had a fit of nerves. I'm made like that, it's my nature. There's nothing I can do about it, it's just life. . . .' And he returned to the German strong verbs.

Ever since then I have understood that strength, intelligence, stupidity, beauty, cowardice and weakness are situations and roles which sooner or later happen to everyone. Anyone who dishonestly appeals to the mischance of life or of his own nature will, whether it be an hour later or a year, be repaid in the name of those same ineffable reasons.

In education we are playing the long game.

REFERENCES

Kohlberg, L (1971) 'Stages of Moral Development as a Basis for Moral Education', in Beck, C, Crittenden, B and Sullivan, E (eds) *Moral Education*, University of Toronto.

Magris, C (1990) *Danube*, translated from the Italian by Creagh, P Collins Harvill, London.

National Curriculum Council (1990) *Curriculum Guidance 8: Education for Citizenship*, York: NCC.

Piaget, J (1972) *The Moral Judgement of the Child*, London: Routledge.

Chapter 11

Providing a Moral Education Independent of Religious Beliefs

Jon Nuttall

The Education Reform Act places a responsibility on schools to provide a broadly based curriculum to promote the spiritual and moral development of pupils and prepare them 'for the opportunities, responsibilities and experiences of adult life'. Before considering how schools are going to make these provisions, let us dwell for a moment on the need for such provisions, focusing in particular on moral education.

The rapid pace of scientific, medical and technological change has affected our lives in many ways. In order that today's pupils are prepared for participation in such a world it is clear that they need, among other things, knowledge and understanding of scientific processes and skills to control them. However, there are further, less direct but no less important ways in which our lives have been changed. The solving of technical problems often gives rise to problems that demand different sorts of knowledge and understanding for their solution: for example, our increasing control over life and death has changed attitudes and presented new problems. Medicine now provides many ways of postponing death but presents the problem as to whether, in some cases at least, the patient is not better off dead. Science and technology have not produced magic cures: given that the resources available are limited, we have to make choices as to how these are to be allocated. Take, as an example, the control we have over conception and pregnancy: we have the means to allow women to give birth when previously they would have been unable to do so and, equally, the means of detecting abnormalities before birth. The advances in birth control give sexual freedom to women as well as men but present them with new choices. Again, we may have solved the medical problems but in doing so we are presented with the moral problems. Part of preparing pupils for adult life must be providing them with a moral framework within which they can grapple with these and the other problems they will encounter.

Let us therefore turn to the question of exactly how the spiritual and moral development of pupils is to be promoted and how they are to be prepared for the responsibilities of adult life. In its publication *The Whole*

Curriculum the National Curriculum Council (1990) recognizes that the National Curriculum cannot provide the necessary breadth to fulfil these requirements: it can provide only a foundation, which has to be augmented by RE, a range of cross-curricular elements and additional subjects. I am going to consider each of these in turn.

In the same document the National Curriculum Council distinguishes between different cross-curricular elements: *dimensions*, *skills* and *themes*. The idea of similar skills, such as those of numeracy, being needed in different subject areas is unproblematic and need not concern us here. Of the other two elements, consider first the cross-curricular dimensions, which, according to the Education Reform Act, should permeate every aspect of the curriculum. The National Curriculum Council pick out two such dimensions: a commitment to providing equal opportunities, and preparation for life in a multicultural community. However, although saying that there are such cross-curricular dimensions may serve to emphasize the issues that the NCC thinks are important (and surely there are other issues as important as, if not more important than, equal opportunities and racial prejudice), it does not bring us any nearer to providing a moral framework. It really is saying no more than that different topics in different subject areas can be linked together in ways other than the natural, or stipulated, order in which the subject develops.

In fact, the NCC booklet seems rather confused on the matter of cross-curricular dimensions. When talking about preparing pupils to live in a multicultural society it talks of introducing an element, namely a multicultural perspective, into the curriculum: viewing the world from different standpoints will, it is hoped, assist in the development of tolerance and the breaking down of prejudices. However, in talking about equal opportunities it deals not with an element that could be introduced into the curriculum – such as an element that enables pupils to appreciate the need for justice – but with making the curriculum itself available to all. Clearly there may well be things that schools need to do in order to ensure that pupils have access to the curriculum, but this should not be seen as a dimension *of* the curriculum. Moreover, drawing attention to the problem of availability does not help with the problem of what should be in the curriculum.

The cross-curricular themes appear more promising if we are looking for a major contribution to moral education. These themes include health education and education for citizenship. Under the former might appear components dealing with the use and misuse of drugs, sex education and interpersonal relationships, family life and concern for others. Education for citizenship deals with the more public aspects of morality: with rights and duties, with the wider community, with the law and our democratic system.

However, although we find in these cross-curricular themes reference to the sort of concepts that should appear in any attempt at moral education, these themes remain just that – they are subjects about which the teacher can speak and the pupil think. No doubt, speaking and writing about such subjects will promote the pupil's moral development, but is this sufficient? In particular, *how* is the pupil expected to think about such issues? Is he or she expected to come to a decision or is thinking about such things enough? The notion of adult responsibilities seems to imply that a decision is required, since thinking without reaching any decisions is not enough for the exercise of responsibilities. Then is this decision supposed to be reached in an arbitrary fashion or is it necessary to provide an overall moral framework within which moral choices can be made?

A child's education that does *not* provide the child with a moral framework – and I mean a framework and not a set of answers – is a grossly inadequate education. Providing cross-curricular themes cannot, in itself, provide such a framework, and it is perhaps with something like this point in mind that *The Whole Curriculum* admits that the cross-curricular elements 'are significant but do not encompass all Ⅹ that is PSE'.

If we are looking for something to provide a framework for moral decision-making within the basic curriculum, and not simply a context in which moral issues arise and moral concepts are used, then it would be natural to look to RE. The Education Reform Act does not provide for national criteria for RE in the way that it does for the foundation subjects, but it does attempt to strengthen the position of RE in schools by placing a duty on each LEA to set up an advisory body (the so-called SACREs) to review policy and suggest changes needed in the syllabus for RE. Can we be satisfied that RE is capable of providing a moral framework? The first problem that may strike one is: how does RE cope with differences in religious beliefs?

The Education Reform Act (DES, 1988) recognizes that we live in a multicultural society and that in some areas religious beliefs other than those of Christianity predominate. Thus although the RE syllabuses must 'reflect the fact that the religious traditions in Great Britain are in the main Christian' they should also take account 'of the teaching and practices of the other principal religions represented in Great Britain'. Thus while the Church of England is represented on the SACRE, so also are Christian and other religious denominations that reflect the principal religious traditions in the area. These provisions attempt to cater for religious groupings other than the Church of England that achieve majority status within an area. Nonetheless, there will remain areas that are predominantly C of E within which RE does not reflect the beliefs of minority religious groupings.

By delegating the provision of a moral framework to RE – and if this has not been delegated to RE, then there simply is no arrangement for providing pupils with a moral framework – the implicit assumption is made that such a moral framework can best be provided (or perhaps, can be provided only) by a set of religious beliefs. For the majority, it is the Judeo–Christian tradition, as found in the Old and New Testaments, that will provide the moral framework. Where other religious beliefs predominate, one assumes that these will provide alternative moral frameworks. We may well feel that it is not the job of the state to change the religious beliefs of a child from a different cultural background, and indeed it is thought that those involved with religious education should promote 'respect, understanding and tolerance for those who adhere to different faiths'. But can we accept that the state should not have anything to say about the moral beliefs that are embedded in these religious beliefs? There appears to be a certain complacency in supposing that we can leave a pupil's moral development to RE.

However, my primary concern is not with those children who have different religious beliefs from the supposedly prevailing Christian beliefs or who come from different cultural backgrounds; my concern is with those children who have been brought up within our culture. It does not follow that because the religious traditions of this country are Christian and the majority of children are brought up, in some sense at any rate, within these traditions, they therefore embrace Christian beliefs. It would be difficult to answer the question as to how many children do believe in a Christian God but there must be at least a significant minority who do not – and not because they have some other religious belief but because they have none. Can RE based on Christianity (or indeed, on any other religion) provide a moral framework for such children? If it cannot, then we are still looking for something to provide a moral framework for many of our pupils.

The assumption often seems to be that it can, that the Christian faith contains not only a set of religious beliefs concerning man's relationship with God and God's embodiment in his son, Jesus Christ, but also a set of moral beliefs clearly put forward by Jesus. The religious and moral beliefs of many people *are* interconnected: it is generally considered that one test of the sincerity of someone who is converted to Christianity is the extent to which their life is changed and they follow, or at least strive to follow, the moral teachings of Christ. On the other hand, there are also reasons for thinking that the moral teachings can be detached from the religious beliefs: someone who loses his or her religious beliefs might still retain the moral framework. Yet this is by no means inevitable; such a person may instead come to believe that there are no longer any reasons for living the moral life of a Christian. Sometimes such a rejection of Christian morality is followed by the adoption of an alternative moral framework, sometimes by the feeling that there is no such thing.

Assuming that I am correct in saying that RE cannot, in general, provide a moral framework for those pupils who do not share the religious beliefs on which it is based, we are left with additional subjects to augment the National Curriculum and thus provide a pupil's moral framework. What additional subjects are on offer? The obvious choice is Personal and Social Education (PSE). But to talk of PSE is to highlight the problem, not to give a solution. We are trying to discover *how* we provide personal and social education. The answer that I am going to propose is that a major element should be philosophy – in particular, moral philosophy.

The first problem to overcome is the image that people have of philosophy. By philosophy I understand a process of analyzing arguments, questioning assumptions and mapping out the logical relationships between concepts. As stated, this sounds rather dry and academic. Much philosophy is indeed taught in a dry and academic way, but it need not be. The popular view of philosophy (in as much as there is a popular view – and this in itself says something of the neglect of philosophy) is of going around in circles, endlessly qualifying, hedging one's bets and failing to come up with 'the' answer. It is true that philosophy does not come up with easy answers, but it is equally true that many of the questions that puzzle us (children and adults alike) in relation to moral issues are philosophical questions. If we lived at a time when there were few problematic moral questions and little in the way of disagreement over moral issues, then arguably philosophical questions would not seem so pertinent. However, for the reasons already given, there is much scope for moral disagreement and an urgent need to find some firm ground on which to base moral decisions.

I want to stress that philosophy (as I see it) does not set out to offer an alternative set of beliefs to those provided by Christianity. Philosophy and Christianity (or any other religion) are not in conflict. I do not, for example, see philosophy as putting forward a set of metaphysical beliefs nor a set of humanistic beliefs. Philosophy does not offer a set of beliefs at all: at best it provides the skills for evaluating a set of beliefs and for exploring the consequences of holding certain beliefs.

In order to see the tasks to be performed by the teaching of philosophy within a PSE course, let us examine somewhat more critically the role that religious beliefs are supposed to play in supporting a moral framework. We can suggest that they do this in two ways: (a) by providing an objective viewpoint; and (b) from this objective viewpoint indicating which would-be moral beliefs are correct and which incorrect. In rejecting the religious beliefs the child is, at the very least, likely to reject the particular moral teachings that are linked to them. At worst, the child is likely to reject the whole idea of an objective morality and instead believe that there are no objective values, that what is taken as right and wrong is just a matter of opinion. (In this, the child might be supported by some philosophers!). I believe that it is possible to argue for an objective basis for morality and that, at the very least, the teaching of philosophy will benefit those pupils who reject the moral ideas along with the associated religious education. In fact, I want to make a much stronger claim: namely, that it will benefit the majority of pupils and not merely that 'special needs' group of non-believers. In order to make this claim plausible, I need to suggest the sort of approach that might be taken. Since philosophy is an activity or a process, the only way that I can do this is by doing some philosophy. Given limitations of space, the arguments will be very sketchy, but if the effect of this is to stimulate disagreement and discussion, so much the better.

The first issue to be addressed is that of objectivity. Traditionally the Christian God, omniscient and omnipotent as he is supposed to be, represents the objective viewpoint. My view of the world may be different from yours. God's view of the world, however, is not just one more view of the world, it is the view of the world as it really is. If there is such a viewpoint, it becomes possible to say whether my view of the world, or your view, or neither, is right. God provides the objective view against which subjective views can be measured.

God is not only omniscient and omnipotent, he is also good – that is, perfectly good. Hence, God's view again provides the objective viewpoint, this time the objective viewpoint on morality. I might have my opinions as to what one ought to do and you might have your opinions. Without an objective viewpoint, neither set of opinions is better than another. However, for the Christian who believes in a perfect God, those opinions that conform to God's are correct and all other opinions are incorrect.

To explore the question of whether the notion of objectivity in relation to moral issues makes sense supposing that God does not exist, we can follow several different, but complementary, lines of enquiry. First, we consider why the notion of objectivity makes sense in relation to what would generally be called matters of fact. Different people may have different opinions on factual matters – whether the earth is flat, whether smoking causes cancer, whether the universe started with a Big Bang, and so on – but we do not think that one opinion is as good as another. One can then explore the criteria we use for saying that one opinion is correct and the others incorrect, what we would need to find out in order to settle a dispute. These criteria are likely to be different for different types of disputes but the notion of agreement and public testability will turn out to be important. The discussion can then be extended to disagreements about moral matters: what evidence, if any, will settle disagreements? Many disagreements are the result of a lack of information – for example, two people may disagree because they have made different assumptions as to a person's motives. From here one might move on to consider whether a supposed distinction between facts and values is justifiable – many philosophers have thought it is – and, if so, whether this distinction corresponds to a distinction between objective and subjective.

A second line of enquiry is to see whether pupils really do think that all moral judgements are simply opinions, which are all equally good. One can start by discussing matters where one would expect to find disagreement and matters where they would think that their opinions differed from those of many adults – sexual morality and interpersonal relations are obvious areas. One can then be provocative and throw in for consideration various extreme sexual perversions, child abuse and so on. One may then move on to consider the sorts of behaviour that the overwhelming majority, if not all of them, would agree were wrong – cases involving torture, cruelty and so on. These can be brought home by using examples from newspapers. If they are not prepared, in these sorts of cases, to allow that all opinions are equally good, then one can start exploring why some opinions were wrong. One might suggest, for example, that there is something wrong with a person who cannot see that cruelty is wrong (perhaps in the same way that one would say that there is something wrong with the person who cannot see that pillar-boxes are a different colour from grass). In this way one would hope to establish that, at least for some issues, what is morally right is not simply a matter of opinion, that all opinions are not equally valid and even that one cannot allow that others are entitled to their opinions and to do what they think right. This would not show that the same applied in all moral issues but it would at least provide the basis for a moral framework.

The second issue, after the consideration of objectivity in moral judgements, concerns reasons as to why we should behave morally. Religious beliefs provide such inducements, whether they are based on fear or love of God. Children who do not believe in the existence of a loving God watching all that they do, and who reject talk of heaven and hell as no more than a fairy story, might think that they therefore have no reason to do anything other than what they please or think they can get away with. A moral framework must at least provide a reason for acting other than fear. In the first place, it can be pointed out that acting morally is not just a matter of doing the right thing, it is doing the right thing for the right reasons. Thus someone who helps others just in order to be rewarded or who keeps the rules just because he or she is afraid of the consequences of breaking them is not really a morally good person. We might explore why it is better for people to do the right thing for its own sake rather than, say, out of fear: namely, that a person who does the right thing only out of fear will continue to do the right thing only for as long as he or she is afraid.

So what reason does a person have for doing what is morally right even when doing so conflicts with self-interest? There are two ways of

172 Education for Citizenship

answering this sort of question. The first is to deny that acting morally is against one's self-interest – an extension of the idea that honesty is the best policy. Thus, when it is the case that doing something appears to go against one's interests, this may be because it is against one's short-term, but not long-term, interests; or it may be because it is not what one desires to do, although it is what is better for one – what we want to do is not always what is best for us and sometimes we may not know what is best for us. Sometimes it may be that although the direct consequences of an action are not in our interests the indirect ones are.

There are two separate ideas here. The first is that human beings are better off living in a community than living as isolated individuals. Within a community, people support each other in such a way that everyone gains, but as isolated individuals everyone else is an enemy. If we accept this point, morality can be seen as a set of rules to make society work. Then, since one gains by living in society, it is in one's interest to follow the rules of that society, even though this sometimes means acting in a way that appears contrary to self-interest.

There is another, more radical, way in which one might suggest that acting morally is, contrary to initial appearances, in one's own interests. This stems from the idea that, in pursuing only self-interest, one loses what one is trying to obtain, that the happiness one is seeking is not to be found in this way. Thus one can explore the idea that people who live a good life, who do the right things, who live virtuously, are more satisfied, more content, more at peace with themselves, and so, although they may have less in the way of material possessions, they are in fact better off. In both these ways, morality can be seen as enlightened self-interest.

Alternatively, we can explore why it is that we think one has a reason for doing something that is in one's own interest but not for doing something that is in another person's interest. If my experiencing pain is undesirable, then is it not equally undesirable for others to experience pain? As well as having a concern for ourselves do we not also have a concern for others? Is it not natural to feel sympathy for others and does this feeling of sympathy not give us a reason for helping others as well as helping ourselves? Perhaps through knowing ourselves better, we can discover within ourselves reasons for acting in a morally good way.

When it has been argued that, even if there is no God, it does make sense to talk about objective moral standards, and there may be reasons for doing what is morally right, even when this runs counter to self-interest (at least, when this is conceived in too narrow a way), the third issue is to explore ways of arriving at morally correct decisions. Given that there is debate and disagreement, over some moral issues at least, and that sometimes we are faced with moral dilemmas for which there appear to be no easy answers, how do we decide what we should do? Again, there are a number of complementary approaches.

In the first place it should be recognized that a moral decision is not simply a decision about that particular case, it is a decision about other cases that are relevantly similar (although, in practice, what counts as relevantly similar is not always easy to judge). Another way of saying this is that, if my judgement as to what to do is a moral judgement then I must be able to give a reason for it, even if I am not able to formulate this reason very precisely. In this respect, moral judgements are different from likes and dislikes. It does not matter that I am unable to say why I don't like tea or why I support Manchester United, but I must be able to give a reason for the moral judgements I make: it's wrong because it is lying, it's right because it will make her happy, and so on. (It may not be so easy to give reasons for the reasons – What's wrong with lying? What's good about making people happy? – but this is a different point: reasons must come to an end somewhere.) What this means is that, once we start to make moral judgements, the effect snowballs, since the judgements we make entail all sorts of other judgements. Thus by thinking about those issues that we are clear about, we may be able to arrive at general principles that can be applied elsewhere. Some philosophers have likened this process of developing a moral theory to that of developing a scientific theory, with principles being obtained by generalizing from particular moral intuitions and then being tested against further intuitions: a mismatch may cause us to modify our principles or, in cases where the principles are particularly well established, we may want to rethink our intuitions, since feelings can lead us astray.

However, there are other ways of generalizing. By considering particular cases we may distinguish between the different features that are relevant to our moral judgements. For example, we may consider the consequences of an action: does it benefit anyone, does it cause people pain, how many people are affected, are a lot of people affected a small amount or are a few people greatly affected? What were the motives or intentions of the person carrying out the action? Was he or she doing it for the right reasons, were the consequences foreseen, and if they were not foreseen, should they have been? How was the action carried out: carefully, deliberately, casually, unwittingly?

Alternatively, how would we describe the character of the agent: mean, happy, cowardly, spiteful, generous, forthright, deceitful? These are descriptive terms but they are also morally loaded. It may be that when there are disagreements between people it is because they are giving different weights to these different considerations. It may be that when one is uncertain how to judge an action it is because one is being pulled in different directions by its different aspects. Becoming aware of these may at least make it easier to see why the decision is a difficult one or why there is a disagreement – in other words, it becomes clearer why judging right and wrong can be a complex matter. Revealing the complexities of moral issues is an important part of providing a framework from which to view moral issues.

It may be said that the sorts of considerations that I have raised in this very brief exposition of the lines along which moral philosophy could be developed are difficult and sophisticated and too advanced for children of 16 and under. Such a criticism, however, does not stand up. In the sciences, children are being exposed to ideas and arguments that not long ago were the stuff of post-doctoral papers; set theory, which once was found only in mathematics degree courses, is now taught to six- and seven-year-olds. In English literature, to take a different sort of example, pupils have to grapple with the moral issues that arise in novels, plays and poems. It is, perhaps, peculiar to the British educational system that philosophy is seen as such an exalted and difficult subject. In the United States, Matthew Lipman has devised ways of teaching philosophy to children of all ages, including children of low ability from deprived backgrounds – that is, to just the group that one would expect to find philosophy most difficult and least relevant. If something is important, it is the job of teachers to make it accessible to our pupils; encouraging pupils to think critically within the context of philosophical problems that are relevant to everyday life is something that *is* important (Lindop, 1990).

A final point that must be made, perhaps in parenthesis, is this. I have been suggesting that philosophical arguments can be put forward to show that morality is not merely subjective, that there are reasons for acting other than in one's own self-interest, that inferences can be made from some moral judgements to others, and so on. Now it would be dishonest to imply that these arguments are conclusive or generally accepted; they are not. Some of the questions to which I have glibly proposed answers have been around for over 2000 years; if they had received a satisfactory solution, they would no longer merit being called philosophical problems. It may be that some pupils will arrive at conclusions that are diametrically opposed to the ones for which I have been arguing. However, if they do so on the basis of a careful weighing of the arguments, then, although I might continue to think that they are mistaken, I must accept that there is a genuine disagreement. But to admit this is to admit no more than that I am in the business of educating rather than brainwashing. If pupils are capable of examining arguments carefully and viewing a moral issue without prejudice, then I am satisfied with their moral development and satisfied that they are capable of exercising adult responsibilities.

REFERENCES

Department of Education and Science (1988) *The Education Reform Act*, London: HMSO.

Lindop, Clive (1990) 'Cultural Thinking and Philosophy for Children', *Cogito*, **4**, 2, pp 50–54.

National Curriculum Council (1989) *Curriculum Guidance 3, The Whole Curriculum*, York.

Index